UNIVERSITY OF CHICAGO STUDIES IN LIBRARY SCIENCE

DIFFERENTIATING THE MEDIA

DIFFERENTIATING THE MEDIA

Proceedings of the Thirty-seventh Annual Conference of the Graduate Library School, August 5–6, 1974

Edited by LESTER ASHEIM *and* SARA I. FENWICK

THE UNIVERSITY OF CHICAGO PRESS
CHICAGO and LONDON

THE UNIVERSITY OF CHICAGO STUDIES IN LIBRARY SCIENCE

The papers in this volume were published originally in the LIBRARY QUARTERLY, *January 1975*

THE UNIVERSITY OF CHICAGO PRESS, CHICAGO 60637
THE UNIVERSITY OF CHICAGO PRESS, LTD., LONDON

© 1975 by The University of Chicago. All rights reserved
Published 1975
Printed in the United States of America

International Standard Book Number: 0-226-02964-6
Library of Congress Catalog Card Number: 74-28809

CONTENTS

Lester Asheim
Introduction   1

Frances Henne
Content versus Container Orientation   13

Ron Powers
The Medium and Three Messages: Perceptions of a Televised Debate   27

Donald R. Gordon
Print as a Visual Medium   34

Virginia Wright Wexman
The Transfer from One Medium to Another: *The Maltese Falcon* from Fiction to Film   46

Wesley Doak
Administrative Problems and Their Solutions   56

Sara I. Fenwick
Summary   67

The Contributors   73

INTRODUCTION

Lester Asheim

In the introductory pages of the Conference program—which also served as an advertisement in advance of these formal meetings—it is suggested that "the most important questions concerning the several media may no longer be those that still seem to dominate the literature of librarianship." We were referring, of course, to the either/or, book/nonbook kind of debates and their holier-than-thou rhetoric. This Conference, instead, assumes that it may be taken for granted that libraries, as centers of communication, will be multimedia agencies in this indisputably multimedia age, and the question should not be which one medium is the best, but rather for what purposes is each medium best? If that be so, we suggest that what does need exploration is the nature of each of the several media, each in its own terms. And from that it follows that the analysis of the proper use of each medium must be based upon standards relevant to *it,* not to some generalized single standard derived from another medium.

The focus of the Conference, then, is upon identifying those characteristics—technical, aesthetic, social, and psychological—that determine the effectiveness of each medium for different kinds of content for different kinds of users and for different kinds of purposes. "Out of this objective and unpolemical emphasis," as the program presents it, "we hope to make a useful first step towards realistically and fairly differentiating the effectiveness of each medium in providing the information, education, entertainment and intellectual stimulation that are wanted and needed by the several publics that libraries serve."

Thus, in broad and—we thought—clear-cut terms, we defined our aims and, in effect, our most likely audience. The aims we saw as quite specific. The audience we saw as very broad indeed.

Now it is notorious that people who are formally and officially concerned with the art and process of communication are the ones who have the most difficulty in communicating. I like to think that this is not because we are even less adept than others in performing the communication act, but rather that we may be more sensitive to communication failures when they occur. Like the city which keeps the most complete police records and therefore seems to have more crime than any other, I want to believe that the popular image of the inarticulate communicator derives not from more communication failures, but from his more complete awareness of them. Whatever the cause, I think the response to our Conference publicity illustrates something of the problem.

Our major difficulty lies in the term "media," which carries a variety of connotations depending upon the special outlook or practice of the group perceiving the term. We tried to indicate the usage to which we are committed by specifying those media with which we are concerned: the broadcast media in their several forms (i.e., radio and television); the film, both as an art form and as a communication carrier; and the media of print in both traditional and new contexts. More specifically, we tried to suggest that our focus would be on content, and the influence of the particular medium upon the content it can most effectively carry, and not on gadgetry or technical operations as such.

Yet—predictably—the immediate response of many who were exposed to our press releases was to think of "media" in a variety of other contexts. There were those media specialists whose emphasis is on the apparatus rather than on the content, who clearly thought our Conference would provide them with a chance to see new devices and learn how to run them. This is a perfectly legitimate objective, but it is not—this time—ours.

There were those to whom the "new technology" means reprographic and miniaturizing devices, and who thought we would most certainly include discussions of the use of microfilm, microfiche, and the like. To our way of thinking, this kind of format is not so much a new form of communication as it is a way to solve certain problems of book acquisition, storage, and cost. A book page is still a book page, however much it is reduced for storage purposes. Our concern is with those media which create new content—and under this heading we would include those uses of one medium which record the content of another, but in the very act of so recording it transform it into something else. Filmed plays are of this nature; the medium interposes itself between audience and content and transforms the product. This will indeed be one of the areas of our exploration, for it is central to our concern about whether the one is truly a substitute for the other. Where it is not, we have a phenomenon amenable to the kind of analysis that we are proposing.

There were those whose interest in "media" focuses strictly on *non*book devices, ignoring completely our warning that the book is one of the media to which we would pay particular attention, stressing by our very attention to all the media that which is unique and indispensable in each of them, the book included.

There were the proponents of the learning-resources approach, who include in their concept of media study carrels, language laboratories, and a world of "realia," from live hamsters to dead leaves, which never for a moment had, I must confess, occurred to us, although we accept without question the communication and educational role that they can play.

And there were those to whom media means, quite specifically, *not* the major commercial channels of mass communication, whereas—in our own private understanding of the term—it was those very media which presently constitute the major commercial channels with which we hope to be much concerned.

I have carefully tried to word that last sentence—"those media which presently constitute the major commercial channels"—to suggest an important distinction, between the medium itself (film or television, for example) and the commercial-channel application of it. Film and television need not be, as you are all well aware, simply mass commercial media; they are forms of communication capable of quite small-scale, noncommercial, private or artistic or educational uses as well. What we do suggest, however, is that whether on a mass scale or in intimate face-to-face use, the effectiveness of the message carried on such a medium does indeed depend upon adaptation of the content to that medium. Thus, in the production of a film, let us say—whether by Hollywood or the kid next door with his hand-held camera—the way the medium is used will affect the impact of the communication experience. We were pleased to see in the special section on "New Media Publishing" in *Publisher's Weekly* last June [1] a report that makers of educational films had, as a result of the decline in the use of their traditional products, come to a new insight. What they had decided is that artistic use of the medium is more effective and desirable than "instructing" in a heavy-handed manner; their new look will be to create good *films*, which will make their point more effectively precisely because they are *good films*.

This conviction, apparently somewhat reluctantly arrived at by the information industry, is the basic theme of this Conference. And the library relevance of this tenet harks back to the mission of the librarian as identified by Ortega y Gasset some forty years ago [2]. In his statement, the librarian was described as a filter interposed between man and the torrent of books. We would today, of course, broaden the concept to read: "a filter interposed between the users of communications and the torrent of sources of communication content," but the idea remains the same: the librarian has a role to play in identifying the most effective means for the dissemination of different kinds of messages to serve different purposes for different audiences. The stress is not so much on the format or the document in itself, but on its effectiveness in meeting the needs of its users, and this imposes a responsibility for selection.

We realize that not all librarians today accept the centrality of selection in the librarian's obligation. In their concern for intellectual freedom, which we share, there are those who see the ideal library as that which has everything, imposing no exclusions for any reason—either quality, accuracy, sound factual authority, or social importance, since all of these elements are subject to personal interpretation.

This approach seems to us unrealistic on two counts. The first is obvious: no library can have every item in every medium, so selection of some kind, by the very nature of budgetary and space realities, must take place. The second reflects what seems to us to be a hidden assumption: that where librarians accept the responsibility for selection they will inevitably become self-serving, imposing their own preferences, ignoring the needs of their patrons, and building an elitist collection that is oriented to administrative convenience rather than service to users. We reject this as an operating premise—which is not to say that it cannot ever happen or that it never has. But any system can be abused by those who would misuse it; it is our hope that we can identify selection criteria which will help to promote user rather than supplier satisfaction, by placing emphasis upon use, not simply collection. And if there is a danger of selector bias in the building of collections, we see it as more likely to be manifested where decisions are based on format rather than where they are based on content related to users.

That is why we have suggested in our program announcement that the continuing confrontation between the hard-sell advocates of the "New Media" and the die-hard defenders of The Book is really no longer fruitful—they are both, in their separate ways, format-oriented. The librarian who would not consider anything unless it is a book (or, more liberally, print) is really no more misguided than the media specialist who will accept anything as long as it is not a book. The criterion in any medium, therefore, is not format *in and of itself;* the criterion should be the value of the content. And we are suggesting that the value of the content is considerably affected by the extent to which the format is properly used in relation to the content and to the needs of the audience to whom it is addressed. Thus we are suggesting that the selection of materials is still one of the librarian's most important functions, and we are hypothesizing that despite their growing hospitality to a variety of materials and not just the materials of print, librarians do not impose criteria of selection with the same rigor when choosing the so-called newer media as they have traditionally employed—or at least used to pride themselves that they employed—in the selection of books.

We are not saying that choice and selection do not take place in the acquisition of the newer media, but we are suggesting that there are two possible directions in which librarians err when they make their selections. One is in the willingness to impose much lower standards on newer media, simply because they *are* the newer media. Many librarians feel that we need more films or tapes or cassettes in our libraries to show that we are in the new multimedia mainstream, and so they accept inept filmmaking, for example, where they would never accept comparably inept writing. Bad writing is a definite mark against book purchase, but poor filmmaking seems seldom to enter as a criterion in the purchase of a film.

Closely related to this error is that of applying to all of the other media criteria derived from the evaluation of literary productions. This may seem to be a contradiction rather than a parallel of the fault of debased standards, but the failure in both cases lies in the application of criteria inadequate to assess the particular medium under review. Librarians of course are, historically, book-oriented, and *book* selection was, for a long time, a staple of library school instruction. Today the title of the course has been changed to "Selection of Materials," but we are guessing that the content and the criteria have been altered very little. A film adaptation of a novel, for example, is judged on its fidelity to the novel, not on its quality as a film. As an illustrative aside, there is a very interesting review of the film *The Great Gatsby* in the *Chronicle of Higher Education* which casts a critical eye on the many angry and bitter reviews of the film by critics whose touchstone is the book. Landon Jones suggests that "there is no way for a movie to carry the full weight of Fitzgerald's symbolism" [3]. I would question this unequivocal assertion, although I would accept his corollary: "The real question is whether *Gatsby* succeeds as a movie." His conclusion is that one should not judge the film by standards of literary art, but rather by the standards of romantic film entertainment, of which *The Great Gatsby* is a quite respectable example. "In other words," according to Jones, "*The Great Gatsby* is not a bad *good* movie; it is a good *bad* movie."

Virginia Wexman will explore in more detail the kinds of problems that are involved in adapting from one medium to another, and will point up more specifically the kinds of conflicts, adaptations, and cross-media equivalents that occur in the transition from one form to another. Suffice it to say here simply that the librarians' book orientation has led us to see all other media as supplementary or subordinate to the book, as our own standard terminology so clearly reveals. "Nonbook," "nonprint," "audiovisual *aids*," we say condescendingly, leaving no question as to which format we place at the heart of the learning process or the aesthetic experience. With that kind of bias, often unrecognized in ourselves, we tend to expect of the other media that which we like best about the book, and to ignore the peculiar strengths and weaknesses of each of the media, including the book, that could help us select more wisely among them.

Selection of materials is less easy than it would appear to be, for a variety of reasons. When we select, we do so on the basis of a considerable mix of criteria: we are interested in subject matter, in form, in treatment, in public demand, in cost, and in a number of these combined. Thus it must be recognized that the selection of each and every film or recording or book may not necessarily be concerned with the art of the particular medium. There are reasons to preserve certain content for purposes other than the art of the carrier. There is a film of Pavlova dancing the Dying Swan, for example, which is an indispensable document of a specific dancer's performance. Its value might be enhanced if it were really a good film, but the fact that it is not does not deny it its place in a dance collection. This kind of record is extremely important for libraries—but having said this, we have said all that needs to be said in the context of this Conference. We are not, in this kind of situation, concerned with the effectiveness of the medium in its own right, but simply with its value as a preserver of something else. This puts it, as an art form, into the class of a Xerox copy or a microfilm, which is not to underestimate its importance or even its social implications.

We are all used to this kind of selection—for the record rather than for the art—but in either case, the peculiar strengths of the medium for carrying particular kinds of content are involved. This visual presentation of the *movement* of the dance is better conveyed by moving picture film than by a film strip or a verbal description, even when the art—not just the attributes of the film—is not involved. A documents collection, a collection of archives, is not limited to those which are well written, but even here the medium may make a difference. No one in 1974 needs to be reminded that an edited transcript is not as good as an unexpurgated tape if what we want is a record of everything that was said *and* the intonations that help interpret meaning and intent. On the other hand, if our purpose is to get a quick overview of the general topics discussed, an edited and interpreted document that cuts out all the repetitions and irrelevancies and interprets the high spots might well be more useful. The nature of the medium employed does make a difference in the use to which the content can be put.

Thus a major concern of this Conference will be this very point: what does the nature of the medium itself do to the content? Ron Powers's paper, concerned with identical content carried in three different formats, explores some of the differences imposed by the medium. Out of this interesting case history should come some useful generalizations as to the impact of each medium for particular purposes, and the reservations one must make about the substitution of one medium as an equivalent for another.

This use of substitute media has been a popular basis for speculation in education these days. Why not get a filmed lecture of an outstanding teacher, the argument goes, and then simply project that in classrooms across the country, so that all classes would have the same educational experience that is now limited to the students in the original classroom? My guess is that Mr. Powers's answer would be that it is *not* the same educational experience. This is not to say that the filmed lecture might not be a useful educational experience in its own right, but it is to say that one is not the equivalent of the other, and that identification of the "best" one depends upon the purpose to be served.

Precisely because we now have a variety of media from which to choose, we can today select content to serve a variety of purposes and users. When the book was, to all intents and purposes, the only format that carried intellectual content amenable to wide dissemination, the book was, indeed, *the* medium of communication, and the librarian was concerned quite literally with finding the right book for the right person at the right time. If the book was not the right medium for some persons, then they could not be served by us. But today they can be, for we are able now to see libraries, not as book agencies only, but as agencies of communication; the standards need not be less strict, but the performance of our task can be broader and more varied. Depending on the nature of the content, the needs of the user, and the ways in which the user wants to employ the content, we can provide it in the book form for one purpose, on film for another, on taped recording for a third.

The value of this new freedom is clear enough where the content differs in each medium. We all recognize that one may wish to listen to a piece of music, look at a painting, but read about the lives of the artists who created them. But already librarians know that they may need all three formats even when the content is ostensibly the same, because each serves at least one purpose or one audience better than either of the other two.

There is no possibility, within this short Conference, to deal with the kinds of technical and psychological problems that we are beginning to approach if we follow this line of thought to its logical conclusion. Experts in the media know a great deal about the ways in which effects are gained through informed use of each medium—but this is knowledge gained over a lifetime of experience, experiment, theory, and trial and error. Filmmakers know, for example, that a wipe from left to right has an emotional effect different from a wipe from right to left; a painter can direct the sequence of a viewer's attention by establishing a kinship between three points of visual relatedness—shape or color—within a composition; the composers of movie music have a bagful of sure-fire tricks to manipulate our moods and emotions in response to musical cues of which we are often not even aware. This is fascinating stuff, and pertinent to our discussion, but we cannot cover everything. We will have to limit ourselves, for the most part, to more general conclusions about the attributes of the several media, and what these suggest as to affects and effects to be expected from them. But this does suggest that selectors will have to be more sensitive to the subtleties and nuances in each format that go beyond the simple description of the dominant subject matter. Donald Gordon, for example, will explore some of the ways, besides the use of language as such, in which print is used to attract attention, arouse emotion, impose a pattern of thinking, and create an atmosphere of receptivity for the verbal message. We may one day have to be as expert in evaluating the work of the compositor as of the author, as we select the materials of print for library uses.

While an in-depth exploration of these specific subtleties is beyond the scope of this Conference, we do not mean to suggest they are not an important part of the approach to media differentiation with which we are concerned. Certainly we are eager to go beyond the fairly simple-minded distinction which points out merely that moving pictures are better for depicting movement than still pictures are. On the other hand, a look at some of the uses to which film is put suggests that even so obvious an insight as that is not always mastered by those who make films or who use the product.

Still we should be careful about jumping to conclusions about the attributes or limitations of a medium. Michael J. Arlen has said: "I used to think automatically that television was primarily a visual medium . . . but I no longer am quite so sure about how visual television really is. . . . It occurred to me . . . that if one had to choose, during most of the hours in which television stations broadcast, and certainly during most of the daylight hours, between having the sounds on one's set turned off and having the picture turned off, it would somehow make more sense, be more useful, more intelligible, to have the picture off, because what you have so much of the time on television is static (almost still) pictures of people sitting down and talking" [4, pp. 23–24]. This use of the television medium may actually fulfill a need felt by many of its so-called viewers, but it certainly does not capitalize upon that which the medium is supposed to do best. The study of television as a medium is not yet sufficiently advanced to determine what it does do best; the experiments are still being carried on by the trial-and-error method of the marketplace. The point to be made here is simply that it is dangerous to come too readily to one-dimensional judgments about the characteristic attributes of a medium; they could lead us to overlook the inventive and creative uses of the medium which move beyond these snap judgments about media limitations.

As an example: One of the great silent films—at least to my mind—is Carl Dreyer's *The Passion of Joan of Arc,* which utilizes a subject which, it would appear on the surface, is a highly unlikely one for film treatment. One setting, very little action, and lots of talk—surely not the stuff of effective silent filmmaking, as some critics were quick to point out at the time. Yet Dreyer knows what the camera can do besides follow breakneck chases; he moves in close on faces, he utilizes camera angles and lighting to probe the nuances of changing facial expression in a way that no other medium could, and he creates—by his use of the qualities that the moving camera alone can achieve—a film of almost unbearable emotional impact. My point is that there are much more subtle uses of each of the media than the usual inventory of attributes provides us, and alertness to these uses is certainly a faculty to be employed in selection.

Study of the media, pretty much in this very context, has come a long way in the field of education. Much of what is now known through educational research is pertinent to our concerns in this Conference —but there are also subtle differences between an evaluation of group use of a medium and individual use; of children's use of a medium and that of adults; and—despite the growing emphasis in the classroom upon learning rather than on teaching—between the in-school and out-of-school experience. Teaching devices and methods, highly successful in the classroom under the kind of controlled conditions that prevail there (even permissiveness is built into a classroom situation) may have the opposite effect when imposed upon an adult, self-motivated learner —and even more, upon a seeker of entertainment, relaxation, specific factual information, or a personal, aesthetic experience. Approaches which really motivate kids in the third grade are not necessarily equally effective with adults on their own. I am not suggesting that we should ignore the findings of educational research, but I am suggesting that we may have to select carefully from these findings those that are truly applicable to a different set of surrounding circumstances.

For example, a great number of the studies which compare the effectiveness of one medium against another—the book against the film or the taped lecture against the live one—have found no significant difference between one medium and another in facilitating the attainment of a wide range of teaching objectives. While this may seem to invalidate the major premise of this Conference, I am inclined to doubt it. In many of these cases, the studies have shown merely that a not very inventive use of one medium is no worse than a not very inventive use of another. The emphasis has been almost solely on the feedback on examinations of certain factual or other readily measurable data—an incomplete assessment of the varied richness of communication experiences. By and large, the purpose has been merely to show that the hardware can be used in teaching, and I guess that there was a time when that needed to be demonstrated. But now let us accept the fact that hardware can indeed be employed in such situations; our concern is with the software to which, until very recently, little attention was paid at all. In other words, instructional uses of the media tend to be more concerned with response rather than with stimulus; with "what the learner does rather than what is done to the learner" [5, p. 859]. But when one is concerned with emotional appeals to adults on matters of social outlook, for example, our concern is less with such behavioral analysis and more with the various types of stimuli.

We are well aware that the points we are stressing in this Conference are not particularly new to librarians. Librarians have been in the multimedia business for a long time—long before it was the popular rallying cry it is today. Frances Henne's paper will remind us of some of the kinds of activities to which librarians have long been accustomed which are not necessarily tied to the formats of print, and which have for a long time applied other criteria than literary ones. But, by and large, these nonbook (there's that giveaway word again) activities have been seen as secondary and supplemental; their purpose has been seen as motivational, and their value has been gauged by the extent to which they can be used to lead people to books. This attitude is changing, and one contemporary library school dean has stated our purpose very well indeed: "We must have, and as educators we must transmit, a far better knowledge than we presently have of the relationship of print, of sound, and of image. We must develop integrated systems that can fruitfully amalgamate all media, understanding the place and power of each within the context of all" [6, p. 64]. We could not have said it better, but it is disturbing to realize that the dean in question, in pursuit of the ideal he has so well expressed, believes that it cannot be attained in a school hampered by the weight of the tradition implied in the term "library"; he has changed the name of his school from "School of Library Science" to "School of Information Studies" in order to be free to take the broader, wider, deeper approach that his statement implies.

We like to think that this new approach is *not* in conflict with the library ideal but a contemporary expression of it, utilizing the new tools at hand to accomplish what is implicit in the traditional objectives. It is true, of course, that many of the older generation of librarians came to the newer media after we had been firmly attached to the book tradition, and that for many of us the newer media simply do not speak as rich a language. But some of us can understand intellectually, if not emotionally and in practice, that this may be a reflection of our own limitations and not necessarily those of the media themselves. We see a new generation of library users coming up who are not so deeply wedded to the literary tradition, and understandably we wonder if we can communicate with them. But do not forget that today's and tomorrow's librarians are part of this new generation too, sharing with them their highly developed skills in the many new languages that are represented by recordings, tapes, films, and multimedia events. We have only to be hospitable to desirable change in library outlook and practice to have it come about; the agents of change are waiting in the wings for their cues.

We are thus speaking about the impact of the multimedia orientation upon libraries and librarians. This means that libraries and librarians are elements in the equation, and therefore they introduce constraints and considerations in the processes of selection and use that may not be recognized if we hold ourselves exclusively to the analysis of media based on the qualities of the media alone. Wesley Doak will deal with some of these librarian-imposed constraints as they affect, both positively and negatively, the library's full use of all media. The identification of difficulties, however, is not an argument for abandoning a good course of action. The challenge lies in surmounting difficulties in order to attain desirable ends. To surmount the difficulties we must know what they are, so that we can balance them against values and potentialities to determine whether it is worthwhile to face the difficulties. It is our hope that the papers in this Conference will make more clear the justification for taking on the task we propose.

Our approach in this Conference is concerned with stimulating a truly multimedia approach; with an attempt, insofar as that is possible, to start all of the media off on the same foot, and to measure the value of each one in terms of its effectiveness for users, and not in terms of historically acculturated preconceptions about format. Whenever a librarian speaks to librarians in this tone, the suspicion immediately arises that he or she is really antibook, and that this is some kind of covert way of attacking the values of print, not only in our own time, but even in their historical context. When—in 1955—the Graduate Library School held a Conference entitled *The Future of the Book*, which suggested that the book format should be seen as a means and not as an end in itself, it became necessary to add an "Afterword" [7, pp. 104–5] to the proceedings volume, to refute a widely disseminated report that the Graduate Library School had assumed the imminent and inevitable demise of the book, which would soon be replaced by movies, television, and mechanical devices, and that, indeed, we welcomed this overthrow of the tyranny of print. Actually the Conference had determined almost exactly the opposite: that the book has had more to say, has said it more clearly, and has preserved it for future consultation better than any other communication device, new or old. But for a librarian even to hit upon a title like "the future of the book" was threat enough to the traditionally book-oriented to trigger a violent reaction.

It is our hope that the intervening twenty years have done away with that kind of automatic defensiveness, and that we are now ready —indeed, more than ready—to weigh the worth of all the media by the kind of standard which will in each individual instance give us the most accurate measure of its qualities. As we have suggested, this may require different standards for each one, if we are to get a true assessment and not a distorted one. It is our belief that the things that the book does best will continue to be apparent in such a comparative study, and that the book is not really threatened because there are many things that our media do better. To find the appropriate uses to which each of the media can be put, and thus not to misuse any of them to accomplish ends to which they are not truly suited, is to enhance the value of each one of them—including the book. And in the context of this Conference, that is the once and future role of the librarian: to act as a filter, as a mediator, as a selector. This is the area of the librarian's traditional expertise, enhanced and broadened but not—in its essentials—altered by acceptance of the multimedia approach to the collection and dissemination of the materials of knowledge, information, and ideas.

REFERENCES

1. Doebler, Paul. "New Films Aim for Leading Role in Schools and Adult Education." *Publisher's Weekly*, June 18, 1973, pp. 57–60.
2. Ortega y Gasset, José. "The Mission of the Librarian." *Antioch Review* 21 (Summer 1961): 133–54.
3. Jones, Landon Y. "Review of *The Great Gatsby*." *Chronicle of Higher Education*, May 6, 1974, p. 8.

4. Arlen, Michael J. *The Living-Room War.* New York: Viking Press, 1969.
5. Levie, W. H., and Dickie, K. E. "The Analysis and Application of Media." In *Second Handbook of Research on Teaching,* edited by R. M. W. Travers. Chicago: Rand McNally & Co., 1973.
6. Taylor, Robert S. *Curriculum Design for Library and Information Science.* Education and Curriculum Series, no. 1. Syracuse, N.Y.: Syracuse University, School of Library Science, 1973.
7. Asheim, Lester, ed. *The Future of the Book: Implications of the Newer Developments in Communication.* Papers presented before the 12th Annual Conference of the Graduate Library School of the University of Chicago, June 20–24, 1955. Chicago: University of Chicago Press, 1955.

CONTENT VERSUS CONTAINER ORIENTATION

Frances Henne

My modest assignment embraces all types of libraries and all kinds of media, with focus on current media developments in the former and on characteristics of the latter. Inasmuch as this topic is concerned with libraries in general, specific details relating to the different types of libraries are not spelled out. Unless otherwise indicated, the term "media" covers both print and audiovisual media.

The container receives emphasis in the first part of this paper; orientation, in the second; and content, in the third. All three key words of the title assigned to me are treated in the General Conclusions and Implications section. Many of my remarks relate as much to mediating the differentiation as to differentiating the media.

The Uses of Media in Libraries

Ongoing Developments
A very brief overview of the library world shows the following major activities on the media scene:

1. Continuation of long-established practices for groups, both within and outside the library/media center, for example, picture book and storytelling programs, with and without audiovisual media; book discussions; club activities; film showings; creative-writing sessions; lectures and forums; special programs; book reviewing (usually by young people); and radio and television programs.

In the case of film showings, the emphasis is now on films as ends in themselves and not as "bait" to lead individuals to reading or to using the library; and on providing opportunities for the viewers to discuss and react to the films.

2. Continuation of long-established media services to individuals for information, advisory, bibliographic, and personal purposes, involving the use of print, recordings, filmstrips, 16-mm and 8-mm films, transparencies, and slides; art prints, art objects, and other realia; talking books; microforms; telephone, teletype, and other transmission forms of communication; facsimile facilities; data banks; and computer programs and systems.

3. A surge in the use of audio- and videotapes, with videotaping (utilizing portable equipment) a common occurrence in libraries and library schools.

4. Much excitement about cable television and a high incidence of reported involvement; similar excitement about the potential of two-way communication between public access or other channels and individuals in the home or elsewhere once economic and technical problems have been overcome.

Emma Cohn, a leader in this field, stated, in a recent conversation with me, that over 400 libraries are involved in video/cable activities: some producing and presenting programs on cable television, others engaged in videotaping as a form of precable planning and preparation for later use, and still others exploring the franchise situation and making plans for library involvements.[1] A few libraries provide reference/information services via cable [2, p. 200].

A burgeoning of the number of periodical articles, books, newsletters, workshops, and professional-association activities, all concentrating on libraries and cable television, further attests the participation of librarians in this field and the significance they attach to its development.

5. In school, college, and university libraries, provision, on a more extensive scale, of a variety of "teaching machines," including computer-assisted instruction, for independent study and other purposes; in public libraries, growing interest, with numerous examples of implementation, in providing machines and specialists to assist individuals in achieving their right to read.

6. Less enthusiasm about remote access because of the technical limitations and the expense of the medium; probably less enthusiasm, too, about random access because of the costs of the equipment and of developing the software.

7. Continuing recognition of the possibilities and potentialities of the home terminal and of the computer console in the home, the library, or both places (this has been continuing now for at least thirty years); continuing alertness about the ongoing developments, experiments, and predictions relating to telecommunications, electronics, automation, and communications satellites, and, on a much simpler yet still complex scale, continuing efforts for the development of national information networks, as shown in the work of the National Commission on Libraries and Information Science.

8. In public and school libraries, awareness and use of individuals as resources, with people resource files and contacts used in a variety of ways for information, counseling, and other needs of library users; and for programs, exhibits, assistance in the selection of materials (not to be confused with censorship), the provision of specialized information, and many other types of cooperation with libraries.

9. In public and junior and senior high school libraries, implementation of the concept of the library/media center serving as an information center about community agencies, services, problems, programs, and

---

1. For a discussion of current and potential uses, issues, problems, and procedures, see [1].

planning; and about human, cultural, social, and other resources in the community.

This trend has extended the range of printed and audiovisual resources provided in the libraries and has expanded their services. In due time, it undoubtedly will create changes in the appearance, functions, and activities of most public library outlets. Parallel to this development is the increase in the number of information centers, minilibraries, and reading and study centers.

One aspect of the community-centered public library is well presented in a description formulated by the Community Media Librarian Program of the School of Library Service, Columbia University, which states that the program

is based on the concept that the public library, because of its highly personalized and individualized service, could be the point where the social agencies serving inner-city communities become humanized and comprehensible for the average citizen. The library, operating in an information management capacity, would facilitate personal access to other services by having the needed information available and by guiding the potential user through the bureaucratic labyrinth. The form of communications used by public libraries in this area is crucial in the libraries' efforts to provide information. The urban poor are heavy users of mass media, particularly TV. To set an effective network of linkages between the people and other agencies in the community, public librarians must be knowledgeable and active in this important field of communication. Its personnel must also be skilled in the use of media in all its formats. [3]

No matter what the size or location of the area served by the library, the current emphasis on the community—the local scene—forms a significant theme in our professional literature, discussions, speculations, and planning and can be found translated into various forms of action in a growing number of situations.

The already mentioned involvement with cable television in public libraries and schools reflects this tendency, too. Two writers of recent articles [4; 5, p. 32], quite independently of each other, have commented to the effect that, whereas broadcast television may have created McLuhan's global village, cable television now returns us to the community. The distinction between the national and impersonal and the local and personal does not imply that one should be excluded because of the other.

10. The recognition of all types of resources and their related services in library objectives and standards.

The history of national standards reflects the expansion of media resources and services in libraries. In the area of school libraries, long recognized by authorities as being in the vanguard in providing multimedia resources and services, national standards, from their beginning, have included audiovisual resources; and, for over a decade, revisions of the standards have supported the unified media program (that is, no dichotomy in the administration and location of print and audiovisual media) for school media centers. Most state standards for media centers in schools follow in the national pattern.

11. An increase in the number, scope, and specializations of reviews covering audiovisual resources.

Despite this long-needed improvement, many limitations remain. Chisholm describes indexes and reviewing sources and, in her commentary, notes that "overall, reviewing services are haphazard and many overlap"; that "many worthwhile media are never reviewed"; and that the indexes "duplicate each other, yet none seems to be totally comprehensive" [6, p. 20]. She recommends several measures that are essential "if selection of media is to be accomplished in a reliable and informed manner" [6, p. 22].

Most types of media used in libraries have inadequate reviewing in terms of coverage and analyses of content, and some areas are quite barren, such as textbooks and other curriculum and instructional materials.

12. Continuation and expansion of audiovisual media production by the library staff and also by library patrons under the general aegis of staff members; and of opportunities for the presentation and showing of original audiovisual media created by local individuals.

Production represents such a widespread activity, taking place in so many libraries throughout the country, that it requires more detailed mention at this point.

The Production of Media in Libraries
Production is heavily centered in audiovisual media. True, some libraries issue publications ranging from bookmarks to scholarly monographs; some encourage children to write and illustrate books or magazines and circulate the finished products; and a few, generally in the instance of creative-poetry groups, provide opportunities for individuals to read their original writings.

In blueprints currently recommended for libraries and media centers, production areas occupy an important place at both building and system levels. Facilities for making transparencies, mounting pictures, duplicating materials, developing photographs, constructing display and promotion pieces, videotaping, audiotaping, and making films and slides are commonly found. In some situations, facilities for printing, televising, and synthesizing sound are available.

The primary purposes for producing materials are directed toward goals that result in creative and other experiences for library users; promotion and publicity for the library; reports and records of community conditions, events, activities, and other information; library orientation and instruction for staff as well as for users; in-service education; library records of programs, meetings, and other activities; case studies; and archives and source materials relating to local history, arts and crafts, and personages. Some librarians have reported participatory, therapeutic, problem-solving, and evaluative values for individuals and groups, including library staff members, derived from creating, observing, or using locally produced media.

There seems to be no question that the production of materials to meet some community needs, to arouse community concern, to record community events, or to report and describe school, library, and other activities in the community constitutes a very vital function of libraries, particularly in public, school, and community college libraries. The librarian as positive activist surely has a role to play in this respect, too.

The production of media, whether by library staff, library users, or a combination of both, requires the assistance of individuals with specialized skills—among them graphic artists and persons informed about the techniques and artistry of crafting films, creating television programs, and videotaping; and the supportive services of technicians. In most libraries today, the availability of these kinds of assistance is quite limited or totally lacking.

Consequently, the homegrown library productions that now abound all too frequently result in strictly amateur productions, be they transparencies, slide decks, videotapes, films, or other media. Their lack of expertise frequently reduces their effectiveness and usefulness. The production of audiovisual materials by library users for assignments, or for innumerable other reasons, may justifiably be amateurish. The learning, creative, and other experiences thereby derived suffice. The guidance of a specialist may not move the productions from an amateur level, but it would help and would enhance the perception and skill of the amateur producer.

Any discussion of our involvement with production must raise the question of copyright in connection with locally produced materials that in one way or another incorporate copyrighted material—print, music, broadcast programs, or other media content. The "fair use" policy that has permitted schools and libraries to reproduce copyrighted materials should not be abused but, I suspect, frequently is.

Orientation

Some Orientation Conditioners
Many years ago, some enterprising researcher identified several hundred purposes that people (collectively) had in reading. Surely, an even larger number would apply if all media were considered. For whatever purpose, known or innate, that a library user seeks media, some general factors affecting his orientation toward media content and container seem relevant to the theme of this conference.

All media must be easily accessible to the consumer. If we subscribe wholeheartedly to the idea of the polymedia library, we must solve the problems posed by the need for accessibility, not only of audiovisual materials but also of any equipment required for their use. Where these are accessible to library users today, the quantity of both resources and equipment is usually extremely limited.

Another accessibility problem to be solved concerns the circulation of audiovisual resources and equipment for home use. For many decades, recordings, slides, pictures, and prints, including art prints with frames for hanging in the home during a long-term loan, have been circulated. More recently, on a growing but still limited scale, games, toys, filmstrips and viewers, cassettes, and 8-mm films have been circulated. Some libraries have rental fees for films. Circulation of expensive films for group showings, usually to civic and educational agencies possessing equipment, is common practice, but usually restricted because of a limited quantity of material available for circulation from most libraries and little or no duplication of titles. Providing raw material and equipment for the production of materials by library users poses problems, too. In many schools and some public libraries, transparencies, film, tapes, and "shooting" equipment for films, photography, and videotaping have been made available to young people, usually for projects under adult supervision.

In due time, the library's philosophy and responsibility in these matters may become clearly defined and the problems of cost and risk of resources and equipment being mishandled may be resolved. Until then, we are confronted with the necessity of recognizing that individual use of any noncirculating audiovisual, print, or microform resources must be done in the library or in media areas served by the library. Unless space and equipment in sufficient amounts are provided and unless the hours when the library is open are extended considerably beyond what now prevails in most academic, public, and school libraries, accessibility to all media is severely restricted. Accessibility may therefore be the strongest factor in determining what media format the library patron uses.

Even in libraries where audiovisual resources are accessible in large measure, selection by and for the user of what he wants or needs is not always a simple procedure. Expert advisory assistance on the part of the librarian is essential. Intermedia shelving, appropriate cataloging, special subject indexes, and computerized retrieval systems provide needed assistance and access to the contents of resources. It may be easy for the librarian or the user to skim through print to determine the suitability of the material, but it is far from easy to skim through most audiovisual resources.

In-depth information of a factual or descriptive nature often involves the use of a variety of print and audiovisual formats. To the extent that each format supplies something relevant and yet different and supplementary, each format should be used. In the case of duplication of content (which is quite possible), the selection of material for the user may best be determined by clearly identifying his need, finding out what media he prefers, and discovering whether he has to have the material for use in the home. I am not convinced that a multimedia mix is an appropriate or desirable answer for most user requests, especially where duplication of content occurs. It is a temptation (or is it a vogue, or are we occasionally mixed up about multimedia mixes?) to overuse this approach, especially with young people.

While we are on this topic, permit me one or two gratuitous comments that deplore the single audiovisual item that, like the "literary" gift annual of old, contains its own motley mix—for example, the film or slide deck with music backgrounds or the film with music, art reproductions, commentary, scenes, and other ingredients—where the effectiveness or aesthetics of each art form is lost, polluted, or bastardized. The use of two or more screens in media presentations can have similar results, compounded by confusion; this approach, as old as the circus, reached its peak in the stroboscopic era and seems dated today.

Library Users' Orientation toward Media

As Pierce stated, "We simply are not built with separate and different communication networks for separate kinds of communication" [7, p. 918]. He goes on to say, "As we know from our experience, man uses all forms of communication simultaneously, and in a supplementary rather than a divided manner. This is reflected in his nervous system and in the results of experiments that psychologists have made concerning the interaction of the various modalities of human communication" [7, p. 919].

These recognized principles form a general background for any consideration of stated preferences and patterns of media users. Partly to gain insight into the use of media of one group of library users (both public and university) and partly to discover the media orientation of some prospective librarians, I made a very informal inquiry of forty-five library school students who were asked to describe the role of media in their lives, to list the media they used frequently and consistently (not a student use pattern), and to indicate any media preferences they might have.

In this group, the number of media formats used on a regular basis ranged from three to thirteen, with a median of six. Books were reported as being used most frequently (by all but eight of the group); other formats regularly used by over half of the group were mentioned in this descending order of frequency: disc and tape recordings, national broadcast television, films (seen at a motion picture theater), newspapers, magazines, and radio.

In indicating preferences, twelve stated that all print was most preferred; eleven others confined their first preference to books, which, in turn, were narrowed by some to a particular type or subject. Recordings (for music) were most preferred by seven; films, by three; and persons, by three. Eight gave equal ranking to two or more media, noting that each contributed equally but in different ways, and one stated a preference for anything as long as it was "nonprint." For those indicating specific preferences, the range was one to six, with a median of three. I found it interesting that persons—that is, personal contacts with people—were mentioned frequently as regularly used media sources, with three individuals placing this source at the top of their list of media most preferred. (Related is the ranking of the telephone as the most important broadcast medium for another member of the group.)

These figures give some indication of the general orientation of the group toward using media but do not reflect the variety of formats or of content characteristics within formats represented in their comments; nor do they show that each person had a completely individualized pattern of media use.

The obvious observation can be made that the same medium content is used by different people for different purposes and that the same purposes of different people are best met by different media.

For example, two-thirds of the group stated that music was very important to them. The music they liked consisted, in the aggregate, of many kinds: classical, hard rock, folk, bubble-gum pop, and others. Some listened only to recordings; others, only to radio or occasionally television; a few wanted their music "live," at concerts or elsewhere; and still others combined two or more of these approaches. Not counted here among media sources, because of the vagaries of rigid definitions, are those respondents who played some instrument or sang, or the person who rated song lyrics (not the music) as a medium of great interest to her. Over half of those holding music as an important element in their lives said that music was used most to provide a background for doing something else. (In two other cases, the sole use of television—any program—was of this background nature.)

One-third of the group expressed a serious interest in art, and the individual combinations of formats and types of media they preferred were quite varied, as were subjects and techniques. Paintings, sculpture (one person considered sculpture a superior medium for tactile communication), and photography (a medium mentioned by several for other than art connections) were mentioned most frequently, but also cited were books, films, magazines, drawings, slides, posters, and buildings.

It is quite apparent that members of this group believed that the museum, the gallery, the concert hall, and the theater (stage, not screen) qualified as distinct media forms (containers) in themselves, without reference to their contents. Could not the same be said about libraries?

When asked what media resources should be in libraries, without exception all recommended a wide range of media. Most of the group mentioned the values of production as part of a library's program, and some cited the desirability of providing space in libraries for creative purposes. A few mentioned the importance of libraries' becoming involved with cable television.

Although members of this group, by virtue of their elected profession, might be expected to be oriented toward media, their patterns of media use are probably representative of many other individuals. Too, like innumerable other people in this country, many were creating media themselves, with still pictures, slides, tapes (for personal correspondence and family records, among other uses), and films predominating.

It may be an erroneous assumption, but it would seem probable that large numbers of people, as consumers of media, have a knowledge of many (not all) audiovisual media that goes beyond the amateur level. Recognition of this factor has done much to remove the "let's show a film" (that is, any film) syndrome in libraries, classrooms, and other places; it has also brought about the participation of young people and others in the selection of films and other media for libraries.

Content

What can one safely say about media content other than it is a vast and complex subject? Placing content within even the most rudimentary media schema gives some indication of the analyses that must be employed in describing and evaluating media and, subsequently, in selecting and using media. Each media item has its own characteristics consisting of: (1) medium or container (print, film, recording, television, realia, and others), (2) format (a few examples: book, magazine, 16-mm film, disc recording, cable television, and object), and (3) content, including type (poetry, documentary film, language record, soap opera, mineral specimen, and numerous other examples), subject and theme, and presentation (style, technique, and audience range). Noting container and format presents no problem; beyond that, the multiplicity of characteristics represented within each of the content categories (and categories within each of those categories!) defies superficial and simplistic description and evaluation. A specialized background knowledge is needed to evaluate a media item in terms of the criteria appropriate to its content.

My comments have been directed toward professional evaluations of media. Personal preferences and uses of media form another context, in which characteristics attached to the same medium may vary among individuals or form other patterns. The end result stresses once again the impossibility of generalizations. The replies from the small group of individuals asked to indicate what media do to and for them reflected this variety. Many print and audiovisual formats and types were mentioned collectively, with several cited by most of the individuals, as forming sources of ideas, perceptions, information, emotions, and inspiration; and as providing stimuli which elicited responses of an aesthetic or imaginative nature. Music (of various styles) was mentioned by several as giving them an incentive to work or just cope; these results were derived from the single or combined use of radio, television, and recordings. Companionship came from television and radio.

In noting other things best achieved for them by certain audiovisual media, the group reported a great diversity of subjects, concepts, and feelings. Only a few examples are presented here:

> *Travel:* films, television, slides, and photographs
> *Movement, pace, and tempo:* films, television, and comics
> *Color:* films, art prints, and paintings
> *Horror and violence:* films and television (news and special programs)
> *Laboratory experiments:* filmstrips and films
> *Facts:* graphs and charts
> *People's faces, postures, and expressions:* television, films, and photographs
> *Impressionism:* painting, music, and films
> *Realism:* films and television.

Television gave a sense of "being there" for some, others commented that the small picture screen gave them a feeling of detachment, and one stated that overexposure to a crisis or other event diminished the impact and desensitized the viewer. In the viewpoint of one individual, television and films were preferred because they portrayed life rather than commenting on it. A love-hate relationship characterized the attitude of many who watched television, but still the medium had its unabashed enthusiasts for all types of programs, including soap operas. Its primary use was for news; indeed, this medium was cited more frequently than newspapers or radio for this purpose. For community news and reports, radio and local newspapers ranked highest.

Several stated that they did not like content "translated" from its original media format or type into another, for example, stage plays and books into motion pictures, television "specials" into books, and live concerts into tapes.

General Conclusions and Implications

From this overview of some media developments in libraries and of some general characteristics and factors affecting content versus container orientation, several conclusions and implications emerge:

1. Our immediate and major audiovisual problems in libraries relate to such matters as evaluating resources, obtaining funds, appointing personnel with specialized and technical competencies, and overcoming technological complexities. The acceptance of a philosophy supporting the polymedia library does not constitute a major problem, because standards and widespread practice reflect our conviction of the values and roles of all media in society and in libraries. (This does not mean that we have achieved our current goals or are complacent about the status quo.)

2. Further developments in regional planning, in information networks, and in structuring those apparatuses,[2] which—through their varied provisions for evaluation, examination, and demonstration—assist librarians in making wise selections from the vast amount of media published, produced, and constructed each year, form key ingredients in achieving optimum provision and use of media in libraries.

3. Due primarily to enthusiasm and a kind of blameless zeal, we often undertake roles and activities relating to audiovisual media that stress container rather than content; that result in amateurism; that make use of materials of mediocre or poor quality; and that waste an enormous amount of professional time in the handling of equipment and in the checking and maintenance of both hardware and software.

4. Many aspects of media involvement require the competencies of specialists. Defining "specialist" to cover the many types, situations, and conditions that must be taken into consideration represents a conference theme in itself, and brief mention of this complicated topic is subject to grave misinterpretation. Keenly aware of these hazards, I have nonetheless mentioned or implied that librarians today tend to be media generalists rather than media specialists; that media generalists can and do perform useful functions; and that their services must be buttressed—at national, regional, state, system, or building levels, or some combination of these levels—by the work of media specialists, each with his own competencies in such areas as evaluation of resources, selection of resources, special services, demonstration, and production. Among the specialists are those knowledgeable about audio, visual, and print literacy; instructional design; computer programming; and the methodology of PPBES, MBO, and other acronyms in the accountability field.

Specialization should be oriented toward content and users, and not toward hardware. A person concerned only with media hardware (unfortunately, too many "audiovisual specialists" are preoccupied in this manner) is not a specialist, but a technician. Critics and evaluators of resources may channel their specializations by type or by subject of content, by characteristics of user audience, and in other ways.

Librarians working directly with library users qualify as media specialists when they have in-depth knowledge of all media formats and types within defined subject areas and appropriate for their audience. Such situations can be found today in departmentalized areas of some academic and public libraries, in special libraries, and in some secondary school media centers that have subject specialists. Elsewhere, if fortunate, we have media generalists. As long as understaffing of libraries continues to prevail at both building and system levels, we will have a woefully insufficient number of media generalists, let alone media specialists.

These comments are not advanced as a plea for introducing either

---

2. For one proposed apparatus, see [8].

new terminology or job classifications and are certainly not a diatribe downgrading current activities and efforts in libraries; they are intended to stress the urgent need to provide a variety of specialized services, some of which are not now available at all and others of which are only rarely found.

5. Professional library education has shown some progress[3] in preparing prospective librarians to be media generalists but has done little to prepare them to be media specialists or to alert them to the concepts, ideas, uses, and technology of communications projected for society in the near future. Instances of continuing education offerings in the media field increase each year, but number, coverage, and availability need to be enlarged. Needed, too, in both initial and continuing professional education programs is expansion in the area of content and use of all media resources. Without extensive knowledge of the resources available for the individuals and groups with whom he works or plans to work, the librarian fails to meet the responsibilities and opportunities of his position.

The requirements of a professional education program covering the full range of media are sobering—among them, the diversity of knowledge and competencies to be represented on the teaching staff, the availability of supportive staff, the amplification of course content, the acquisition of resources, and the expense of equipment—and may well provide impetus to planning, on the part of library schools, for allocation of certain specializations to certain schools and for cooperative or consortium arrangements. Too, the time seems most propitious to explore seriously the possibilities of making our professional education a truly interdisciplinary program.

6. Professional education for teachers and for others using media of all kinds in their occupations has had and continues to have serious deficiencies in the area of media resources, both print and audiovisual. Library schools and departments of library science have a professional and social obligation to move quickly toward rectifying this situation. Teachers must be knowledgeable about the content and use of media in their teaching area and, within the boundary of that area, become media specialists. They should be able to participate effectively in the selection of print and audiovisual resources.

7. The stress on community information and information for the community means effective planning, cooperation, and communication not only among libraries but also between libraries and community agencies, broadcast stations, groups, organizations, and institutions. A community communications council provides strength and support for

---

3. My optimism remains despite the findings that, of forty-two directors of accredited library programs, only fourteen strongly agreed and nine agreed that master's-level candidates should be required to take at least one course in nonprint materials. Of fifty-two directors of unaccredited programs, thirty-three strongly agreed and thirteen agreed that there should be such a requirement [9, p. 159].

the provision, promotion, and utilization of media and assists in avoiding pointless duplication in the production and dissemination of media content.

8. In our enthusiasm to amplify our programs, attract users, and promote audiovisual resources and services in our libraries, we tend, sometimes unwittingly, to relegate print, especially books, to the place of the forgotten medium. Much of our library promotion appearing in print, filmstrip, film, or videotape pays scant attention to print. Today, we may need to push print in ways similar to those created by the need to push audiovisual resources in 1945 and earlier.

This is not to say that everyone is or has to be a reader over and beyond acquiring the skills of functional literacy. Nonetheless, are we not at times guilty of stereotyping "readers" as well as "nonreaders"?

The nature and scope of the print collection might profit from reexamination. Some reduction in the number of book titles recommended by national standards might be in order for some libraries; duplication of many titles and a frequent turnover of titles are essential; and collections consisting largely of paperbacks seem desirable. In most school, public, and community college libraries, the magazine and pamphlet collections need considerable enlargement. The stiff and static arrangement of resources that is now found in most libraries needs vitalization, too.

9. Research that investigates the actual and potential use of libraries and media resources is critically needed.

10. Content and container, of course, are important, but our primary goals are concerned with the people who use them. For decades we have made available—through many media—information, knowledge, aesthetic impressions, imaginative experiences, ideas, and truth. The avenues available to us for continuing and extending these and other important services change and broaden. We have now entered an innovative, creative, participatory, and experimental period. Yes, much work remains to be done to make media resources and services adequately and functionally accessible to library users; and, yes, new developments and directions need to be implemented on a wider scale. But, all in all, we can derive many satisfactions from the current and active library media scene. The enthusiasm, the fervor, the energy, and the genuine desire and dedication to provide superior media services for the individual, for groups large and small, for the community, and for society can be found in abundant measure.

REFERENCES

1. Kenney, Brigitte L., ed. "Cable Television for Librarians." *Drexel Library Quarterly*, vol. 9 (January–April 1973).
2. Moskal, Stephen L. "Programming on CATV: The Joliet Story." *Illinois Libraries* 56 (March 1974): 199–200.

3. *Community Media Librarian for the Inner City.* New York: Columbia University, School of Library Service, 1974. Unpaged.
4. Cawelti, John G. "Some Reflections on the Videoculture of the Future." *University of Chicago Magazine* 66 (November/December 1973): 19-24.
5. Fast, Betty. "Cable TV: Developing Video Awareness through Public Library and School Media Programs." *Connecticut Audiovisual Education Association Bulletin,* no. 27 (1974), p. 32.
6. Chisholm, Margaret E. *Media Indexes and Review Sources.* College Park: University of Maryland, School of Library and Information Services, 1972.
7. Pierce, John R. "Communication." *Daedalus* 96 (Summer 1967): 909-21.
8. Bomar, Cora Paul, et al. *Guide to the Development of Educational Media Selection Centers.* Chicago: American Library Association, 1973.
9. Powell, Ronald R.; Young, Arthur P.; and Flanagan, Cathleen. "Library School Directors and the Master's Curriculum: An Attitude Survey." *Journal of Education for Librarianship* 14 (Winter 1974): 159.

THE MEDIUM AND THREE MESSAGES: PERCEPTIONS OF A TELEVISED DEBATE

Ron Powers

In October 1971, William F. Buckley, Jr., appeared in Chicago for a televised debate with the Reverend Jesse Jackson on the question, "Is America Hospitable to the Negro?" The debate was broadcast on public television as part of Buckley's "Firing Line" series. It was taped at WTTW, Chicago's public-television station.

In my capacity as a television critic for the *Chicago Sun-Times*, I was invited to the Channel 11 studios to witness the debate live, as it was being taped. A day later, I watched the program as it was broadcast as a segment of "Firing Line," complete with theme music and production credits. And a day after that, I listened to an audiotape recording of the debate, which was sent to me by Channel 11.

The October 6 editions of the *Sun-Times* carried my review of the "Firing Line" program. It was titled, "Three Ways of Looking at a Debate," and it differed from my usual method of reviewing a television program in one important way: it took under consideration not only the televised version, but also (a) the live event itself and (b) the audiotape record.

It was this column which Dr. Asheim asked me to use as the source material for my remarks herein. (And I must add here that since I originally discussed the topic with Dr. Asheim, a *fourth* version of that debate has come into my possession: the edited transcripts of the tape. I want to make it perfectly clear that Mr. Buckley's staff complied voluntarily with my request for the transcript, and that I am perfectly satisfied there are no gaps or alterations from the content of the tape.)

Also, I want to acknowledge what will quickly become obvious: my conclusions as to the effects of the various versions of this debate are less scholarly than impressionistic, less clinical than speculative. For instance, my perceptions of the debate as a television phenomenon might have been colored by the impressions I had absorbed from seeing it live. Both these sets of experiences undoubtedly influenced my third confrontation with the content, on the audiotape. And as I read the transcript, more than two years later, those collective memories might have played upon the debate as a linear exercise. So I feel somewhat like a cross between Rashomon and Marshall McLuhan.

But I hope that my remarks will be useful to you for that very reason: they will illustrate that educational experiences *are* influenced by the form in which they are presented—and that, as Dr. Asheim suggested, the identification of the "best" form depends upon the purpose to be served. My experience might suggest a similar experiment, but under more controlled conditions: three, or perhaps four, subjects might be asked to witness a debate, one of them in each of the ways I have described. Their resulting impressions could then be compared, contrasted, and analyzed.

Let me now review my original three sets of perceptions of the Buckley-Jackson debate. The first set was of the live event. I was aware of a predominating sense of *arena* as I watched the taping on a Saturday afternoon at the WTTW studios. I could feel that heat generated by the klieg lights above the two men. I felt an impulse to turn my eyes away from the *harshness* of the lights. And as I looked at the two antagonists, sitting in swivel chairs with their toes almost touching but with oceans separating their ideologies, I sensed a suppressed hostility that could flare at any moment.

There could hardly have been two less similar antagonists. Both men are physically big, and they perspire freely, but the similarities end about there. Buckley, in his aggressively modest business suit and his narrow necktie, was the personification of white American intellectual conservatism. Jackson, hunched forward in a brightly patterned polo shirt and flared slacks, and glowering intently at Buckley, was the black "country preacher" whose economic crusade was directed at the very Establishment Buckley represented.

As the conversation started, the two men seemed engaged in an intense struggle of personal will. In his introduction of Jackson, Buckley noted that Jackson was born in *North* Carolina, and later on said he would begin by asking Mr. Jackson whether he believed there was another country in which a *Negro* minority the size of our own would have a better chance of achieving equality. Jackson responded:

Well, the first thing is I'd like to make a couple of corrections. One, I'm from *South* Carolina—Greenville, South Carolina—as opposed to North Carolina.

BUCKLEY: Sorry.

JACKSON: Secondly, we could better communicate by using *black* at this point of time in history.

It was exchanges such as this—contentious, hostile, wary, semantic —that dominate my memory of the live event. My feeling was that each man felt himself responsible for the honor of his own culture, and that the debate topic was merely a device for a deadly serious game of one-upmanship. Very little, if any, of the *content* of the debate was retained by me as a witness to its live performance. I was preoccupied by the sense of theater.

My second set of impressions was culled from the television screen the following day. And it differed almost diametrically from the first. The selective eye of the television camera trimmed out the setting of harshness and heat; it transmitted no record of the tension between the two men that had existed before air time. What was left was a stylized execution of *pure debate:* two talking heads, one serving up sophisticated questions, the other firing back colloquial replies. I sensed a careful execution of style, of ideas arranged against ideas, or crackling abstract argument. The intimate passion was missing. And in its absence, I felt an access to the *substance* of the dialogue: Buckley arguing that black economic advancement had moved upward through this century in a straight line; Jackson countering that such progress was "in proportion to the agitation" initiated by the blacks.

What had been almost a calculated personal insult on Saturday had ossified into a rhetorical gambit on Sunday. I recall this exchange:

BUCKLEY: By the same token, it seems to me that it is plainly the responsibility of the black leaders to denounce the *counterparts* of the Ku Klux Klan when they show up with black skins. Occasionally in the rhetoric of antidiscrimination, with which I thoroughly sympathize, references are continually made to black skins; and all of a sudden, one finds that these people are pleading exemptions for people just because they have black skins.

JACKSON: You know, I somehow get the impression that you are setting up some parallel between the Ku Klux Klan and the Panthers, which I disagree with. The acute difference is that, you know, both groups have admitted publicly that they don't mind killing for what they believe in. The Ku Klux Klan is willing to kill people to resist change; the Panthers are willing to kill people in order for change to come about.

As a live event, that exchange seemed only a stressed syllable or two away from physical confrontation. On the television screen, it was merely a neat, symmetrical *pas de deux.*

There was another example of how the television screen disarmed an emotional flare-up. After Buckley had expressed distaste that a Black Panther paper portrayed Robert F. Kennedy as a dead pig on the day after his assassination, Jackson retorted: "Interestingly enough, Buckley, one who is not hurting cannot very well tell one who is, how to holler." Live, it was an angry moment. On videotape, it did not seem to matter.

I think there is a reason for this discrepancy of impressions between seeing the debate live and seeing it on television which goes beyond mere repetition. Television watching has taught us that, with a handful of exceptions, what appears on the screen is fail-safe. We know instinctively that Johnny Carson won't swear, that Maude won't streak, that Howard K. Smith won't show up drunk on the ABC Evening News. If any of that happened, we know that the videotape—which stands between the event and us—would be destroyed or at least withheld from the air. The videotape has rendered most of television predictable, has grooved our expectations; and—with the occasional exception of an assassination or an on-the-air suicide—it has defused the threat of violent disorder, which is so much a part of our natural instincts. I think that this defusing is not to be underestimated when considering the emotional impact of information delivered via the medium of videotape.

The third set of impressions was derived from the audiotape, to which I listened a day after the televised version of "Firing Line." Here, too, the distinction from the other impressions was curious and unexpected. The Buckley-Jackson debate came across to me on the tape recorder as *two disinterested voices joining in a quest for truth*. It was hard to tell from listening to the voices that there had been a debate at all. Separated from the two men's faces and their accompanying visual clues, their voices seemed more often than not to approach agreement.

Here are some of the exchanges that remained dominant in my mind after I listened to the tape-recorded version:

JACKSON: One should have the freedom to deal with his choice of unions.

BUCKLEY: Yeah. I agree with you.

JACKSON: You agree with me on this?

BUCKLEY: Yes, I do. I agree with you 100 percent. [Laughter and applause.] In fact, I haven't disagreed with anything you've said so far.

And again:

JACKSON: As I see it, the problem for us is essentially economic. And if the problem is economic, then the solution is economic. And to that extent, we need to begin to start looking at economic alternatives, as opposed to organizational alternatives.

BUCKLEY: I think you're quite right, and I've been saying that quite fervently for ten years. But it's also true that one needs good nature. One needs mutual respect. One needs some faith in the good offices of other people.

Agreement, mutual support, a joint quest for truth—this was the sense of the debate that emerged from the tape-recorded audio track.

It was this third set of impressions, I think, which surprised me the most. The tape recorder corresponded in form to the radio, and until this experience I had generally agreed with Marshall McLuhan's description of radio as a "tribal drum," which "extends people's nervous systems to create depth involvement for everybody" [1, p. 298]. If this evaluation is correct, I should have heard a heightened sense of conflict, a sharper and more emotional involvement in the clash of ideas. My net impressions should have been partisan, not neutral.

In *Understanding Media*, McLuhan wrote: "In the Kennedy-Nixon debates, those who heard them on radio received an overwhelming idea of Nixon's superiority. It was Nixon's fate to provide a sharp, high-definition image and action for the cool TV medium that translated that sharp image into the impression of a phony. . . . Radio affects most people intimately, person-to-person, offering a world of unspoken communication between writer-speaker and the listener" [1, p. 299].

To summarize my three sets of impressions of the Buckley-Jackson television debate on "Firing Line": (a) As I watched the live debate, I was aware of a sense of *arena*, of a visceral hostility that could flare at any moment. (b) As I saw it on television the next day, I perceived a *stylized execution of pure debate*, an access to the substance of the dialogue. (c) And as I listened on the tape recorder, I heard *two disinterested voices joining in a quest for truth*. No winner, no loser, just two men talking. Which of the three sets is accurate? I doubt that any of the three is more accurate than the others. As I said at the beginning of my remarks, I am probably a poor judge of relative merit anyway, since the accumulated impressions of the early experiences doubtless colored my judgment of the later ones.

I think there is a more important question. Some of you may have noticed that in none of the three categories did I dwell at any length on the *ultimate effect of the debate itself*—its resolution, a comprehensive description of its organic development, a detailed synopsis of the major ideas put forth by each man. There is a reason for that. In my opinion, none of the above forms was adequate for the absorption and retention of detailed, abstract information. Had I been a student taking copious notes, instead of a critic taking very sketchy ones, I probably would have retained more than I did.

But even conscientious note taking, I think, is a poor reference substitute for the fourth form of the debate—the printed transcript. Only by reading and rereading the transcript was I able to articulate to myself the essential threads of discussion on the topic, "Is America Hospitable to the Negro?" They were these: Buckley repeatedly supplied statistical evidence to persuade Jackson that American blacks were qualitatively better off than comparable minority groups in other societies. And Jackson, just as repeatedly, refused to be drawn into debate on those terms: he was not, he insisted, qualified as an international expert; he was more interested in judging the American black's progress by the yardstick of what it ought to be.

A reading of the transcript suggested to me that the key remark was not to be found in any of the passages I quoted to you earlier. Though the wording is somewhat vague, its intent becomes clear upon rereading:

BUCKLEY: Is the very fact that as much progress *has* been made (as you have pointed to) testimony to the flexibility of the American system, and its general hospitality to what it is that you desire to achieve?

JACKSON: Well, it appears to be more *hostile* to change than *hospitable*. [A bit later.] So I spend more time comparing America with what America *is*, over and against what America *ought to be*, or even other ideologies.

I think in that exchange lies the essence of the two men's ideologies.

And it is a passage that lay buried beneath several varying layers of emotional response on my part, until a careful reading of the transcripts brought it out.

What does all this suggest about the most effective way in which to store and present information? Some interesting, and curiously hopeful, things, I believe. The phrase, "a careful reading of the transcripts," reminds us all of current events in our national history. For all of the summarizing, paraphrasing, dramatic recitals, and compressed reporting of the White House transcripts that were available on radio and television, the American public ultimately turned to the printed form —newspaper texts and paperback volumes—when it became available. At least serious Americans did, and there were more of them than a lot of people, including President Nixon, had thought likely.

A little more than a year ago, Walter Cronkite told me in a magazine interview that if the Pentagon Papers had been brought to CBS first, he probably would not have recommended airing them—because they were a print, rather than a television, event.

The point of these examples—as well as my own experience—is that, contrary to a pervasive popular fear, television has not heralded the death of linear man, Marshall McLuhan to the contrary. McLuhan has said: "Perhaps the most significant of the gifts of typography to man is that of detachment and noninvolvement—the power to act without reacting" [1, p. 173]. McLuhan made those remarks in a context of scorn for the printed work; he went on to characterize typography as "an embarrassment in the electric age, in which all people are involved in all others at all times" [1, p. 173]. And he argued that the typographic extensions of man brought in nationalism, industrialism, mass markets, and other manifestations of rigid, repeatable precision.

But recent events—and again, I am referring to the Watergate epoch—have made a strong case for the feeling that there is a valued place in human events for this very "detachment and noninvolvement —the power to act without reacting," that McLuhan dismisses. The example I am thinking of is the performance of the House Judiciary Committee in investigating, debating, and reporting out the articles of impeachment against President Nixon. Observers on both sides of the issue generally agreed that the committee performed judiciously, moderately, and with commendable deliberation in reaching its conclusions. And it was obvious that its members based their arguments on an exhaustive *reading* of the tape transcripts, and not on impressions they had gained from televised summaries or *reactions* to partisan pressures.

This is not to say that the printed form of information is free from its own distortions. A transcript cannot indicate such clues as emphasis, timing, inflection, and stress—all of which can change the entire sense of a given passage of thought. A good example of this happened to me recently. I have just completed a series of tape-recorded interviews with Dan Rather, the CBS newsman, for a magazine article. The recordings have been transcribed. On one of the pages, Rather is talking about the increasing costs of presidential elections. One fragment of dialogue read as follows:

RATHER: It was clear in 1968 that a quantum leap forward had been made in the amount of money spent on a campaign. It was clear where a great deal of that money came from.

REPORTER: Where? Where?

The sense you might get from reading the transcript of that exchange is one of the reporter breathless, practically drooling, in his desire to know this choice tidbit of information. As a matter of fact, the tape shows that several seconds passed between the first "where" and the second, and that in the interval, Rather was deep in thought. But in print, the "where-where" makes the reporter seem wide-eyed and sophomoric, which as we all know could not possibly be the case.

So the printed form has its own distortions. In the end, it is up to the person charged with presenting a body of communication to decide whether his goal is to evoke emotion, or impart data to be absorbed in a disinterested way, or perhaps a blend of the two.

I hope that my summary of reactions to the various forms of the Buckley-Jackson debate has been useful to you—and that in any case you have not felt too startled upon hearing a bias toward the printed form from a person who makes his living watching television.

REFERENCE

1. McLuhan, Marshall. *Understanding Media: The Extensions of Man.* New York: McGraw-Hill Book Co., 1964.

PRINT AS A VISUAL MEDIUM

Donald R. Gordon

Most of us regard print as the familiar, comfortable, rumpled dressing gown of communications. We take print for granted. We assign qualities of benevolent neutrality to it when it acts as a vehicle for conveying content. We often think print is a little dull, perhaps even dowdy in the company of other media forms. We assume its predictability, its placidity, and its propriety.

And we are quite wrong. Print in its myriad contemporary forms and formulations is actually a dreadfully activist, opinionated ideologue. It is frequently quite improper, generally unpredictable and, given even cursory attention, anything but placid. Print can be as vulgar as any of our media forms or can mingle convincingly in the company of saints. But to get past the comfortable dressing-gown image to the actuality of print takes some thought, attention, and a few leaps of faith. We have to try to shed the unseeing ease of undue familiarity. We have to try to acquire awareness of ordinarily unnoticed influences and behavior. We have to consider the possibility of trickery played upon our unconscious selves at times when we think our gatekeepers are working best.

There can, in fact, be unnoticed wars going on in which content finds itself at odds with the print medium. Dull books may seem duller, good books may be reduced in effectiveness. Unless we are quite careful, we may blame authors and dismiss content for reasons unrelated to either.

Such efforts can benefit from a three-step approach. First, we can seek a reasonable overview, or review, of the basic characteristics of the medium, seeking with relatively fresh innocence some discoveries and rediscoveries. Second, we can bid to relate such characteristics to operative assumptions about the medium in terms of what it does. And, third, we can attempt to formulate some guidelines for subsequent evaluation of print so that we will not fall into the bad habits of dressing-gown thinking as often in the future.

So, what *is* print?

For our purposes, we can start by asserting that print is a proxy agent. It purports to act on behalf of some people or machines in such a way as to facilitate efforts to replicate their sensory-cerebral experiences. Such replications are fixed, constant, and usually numerous expressions in alphanumeric terms cast as language of one kind or another.

Print also has characteristics that flesh out definition and description more fully.

Print is, for practical purposes, permanent. Once typed or cast or photo-offset or whatever, print replications simply sit there, and sit there, and sit there. Day and night, year in, year out, they are available for consultation both for the edification of their originator and the enlargement of others.

The very sensory-cerebral systems involved in and, to a degree, expressed by print gain enormously from this. Flaws and frailties can be accommodated since time can be selected and used—time to bid for excellence, time to correct errors and interpretation, time to goad oneself to peak performance, time to check and check again. Simple, sitting print is one of our original demand systems.

Similarly, print is finite and orderly in most instances. Content, unless it is to be a large blob, simply has to be sorted out into words and sentences or their equivalents. The whirling, multitudinous, complex, contradictory maelstrom of three-dimensional reality has to be ordered, simplified, clarified, and fixed. Two-dimensional print insists upon this by the rules of process and machines.

And what reliefs this can provide! Hordes of distractions are eliminated. Mind-bending simultaneity is sorted and laid out in clear streams of orderly themes. We can pick our ways along the path of explication, confident that nothing else is going on that we are missing. We can focus wholly and wholeheartedly, and, thanks to permanence, at times when we feel so inclined.

Yet, there is also flexibility in print. The form of the print itself, the setting it occupies, the space around it, the relationships of all three to each other—all these can be varied. Changes in size and shape, color, intensity, punctuation devices both formal and informal, and juxtapositions can be orchestrated within very broad parameters.

As a result, the easements of order can be augmented with all sorts of helping hands. Emphasis, nuance of meaning, emotion, opinion, and priorities can all be expressed. We cannot quite get away with a wholly mindless romp through print, but order and flexibility can make consumption remarkably easy.

Print also possesses the characteristic of universality. All copies of any replication will be essentially the same—from first to last.

Thus, for all users, print content gains from a high degree of stabilization. They can at least start from the same input point. They do not have to worry about atmospherics or the quality of local coaxial cable. They can use, as an original, any of the print copies, anywhere they are available.

Such commonality is reinforced by the inherent discipline characteristic of print. In degree at least, the medium is the least vulnerable to the errors and omissions of partial attention. With other media—radio, television, and film especially—it is possible to gloss along with very low-level attention and still come up with plausible constructions.

This is seldom the case with print. Little if any content can be conjured up by a fleeting glimpse or a half-hearted browse. Print demands quite close attention. Without such attention the end result is usually no meaning—rather than flawed and partial meaning.

Now, let us consider some ambiguities which tend to cast shadows on the largely positive print profile that has emerged so far. Most notably, there are the ambiguities of linearity and of limited sensory engagement.

Linearity, in the sense that Dr. Marshall McLuhan conceives of it, means that the order of print is carried to unrealistic extremes. To be intelligible, print has to flow in a step-at-a-time pattern of letters, words, lines, sentences, and so on. The medium tends to impose its own nature upon its content.

And so, ambiguity becomes apparent. We benefit, as already noted, from the order and constructive discipline of the linear thrust. But we suffer from such artificiality as may be imposed by linearity upon content.

For example, take a sensory snapshot of yourself as you exist right now. Note, wordlessly if possible, the massive, *simultaneous*, multidimensional, and multidirectional orchestration that is involved.

And try to imagine expressing that in print.

On the positive side, if you are really to use print, it is inevitable that you will immediately start imposing an order and a print discipline on your snapshot. In that sense, you will gain in terms of clarity, organization, perhaps even intelligibility.

But you will also lose. The unstated "and then" of the linear construction will emerge to impose artificiality and error upon your snapshot. You will be forced to say "I have tickles (and then), whims and fancies (and then), emotional heaves and surges (and then), finite descriptions of objects and events (and then), memories, . . ." and so on and so on.

Your sensory snapshot will be transformed into a series of stylized, simplistic images—one for each ingredient as you formulate it. The interaction, the simultaneity, the flavor and shadings of your very self will be altered.

Now, in a gross sense we all know this. Our best minds and talents have addressed themselves to the challenge involved for centuries. Print expressions as varied as the Bible and the works of Dylan Thomas or Ezra Pound have sought forms to reduce the burden—the artificiality—of linear expression.

But, for all such efforts, and all such time, we have not really accepted all the consequences of linearity. We have acknowledged a general incapacity, a general predisposition to error. But we have not acknowledged the fundamental implications.

Particularly, we have not acknowledged the change in ourselves. You see, print has been our principal ally and principal repository for several centuries so far as contact, communication, and exchange are concerned. It is the principal medium of record and the principal medium of conception and execution. We link back to our past via print. We throw our faded bouquets to the future via print. We wrestle with our ideas and activities via print—even the ideas and activities of other media.

We are, by and large, creatures of print, expressed and bound together by print.

And we are transformed in the process.

Print, virtually inescapably, is linear. Print is our major and paramount vehicle. Print really cannot change from linearity.

And so, in large measure, we humans have changed.

We, adjusting a step at a time, forging our print alliance, have become linear too. Not all of us, not all of the time, but for most practical, day-to-day purposes we have become sufficiently linear to master quite unthinking ease and familiarity with the patterns and ambiguities of a print culture.

So, because of this alliance we can say print is a medium characterized by order, as noted; characterized by artificiality, as noted; and, perhaps most important of all, characterized by an ability to impose such patterns of order and artificiality upon its users.

Now consider the other major ambiguity: limited sensory engagement.

Print, as we all know, is primarily a visual medium. With few exceptions, print does not convey sounds, smells, tastes, or touches at first hand.

And this, frequently, is a very useful situation. Our sensory-cerebral systems would probably pop like firecrackers if exposed to the full array of sounds, smells, tastes, and touches of our collective human condition. The extremes and the total mass of the horrible, the humdrum, and the heroic all about us are simply more than any of us can bear.

And print spares us that. Such aspects of content are filtered and muted so that, for instance, a parliamentary uproar becomes the traditional expression, "Some Honourable Members: Oh! Oh!" Like linearity, such limited sensory engagement can help clarity, bearability, even intelligibility.

But again, there is a burdensome price, a central ambiguity in the medium.

Sounds, smells, tastes, and touches are presented to us at second hand, at best. Often they are translated into visual approximations. Either way our patterns of behavior are subtly conditioned against primary sensory functions simply because print makes them difficult to explore or exchange with others.

Perhaps it is far fetched, but it may well be that the people-print partnership shares responsibility with other malign forces for the inhumanly deodorized, bland, and untouching characteristics of contemporary print-dominated technological society.

At any rate, we now have a basic statement on what print is: a proxy agent to facilitate efforts to replicate and exchange sensory-cerebral experiences, fixed, constant, alphanumeric, finite, orderly, flexible, universal, highly linear, and predominantly visual.

Now, let us consider operative assumptions. Given forms of print appropriate to such terms of definition, what can we or must we assume about such forms?

One assumption seems to be preeminent. That is, the necessary recognition that print—regardless of content—is a separate and distinct language of itself. Print consists of both a vocabulary *and* of a way of using it, and any expressions cast in the print format must take this into account.

Thus, it can be argued that we have English and Print-English, French and Print-French, Russian and Print-Russian, and so on. And the differences between English and Print-English are as basic as those between English and French.

And, reasonably enough, one must ask, how on earth can this be?

Well, we are dealing with language—vocabulary and a way of using it. So let us try to ferret out the vocabulary and way of using it that are specifically applicable to print.

First of all, we can consider what is not present. Print is neither oral (mouth) nor aural (ear). It cannot really encompass overtones and undertones implicit in oral-aural transactions. I may say "I *love* you" and you may hear "I love *you*," and apart from the gross signals of underlining or boldface or the like, much of the true substance of such oral-aural exchange cannot be conveyed in print.

So, right away, English and Print-English drift apart a bit. A host of shadings, inflections, nuances, and *meanings* assumed and learned in the oral-aural tradition simply do not apply in print. You will find consumption of any print version of even this presentation quite different from such exchange as we may have in an oral-aural mode.

At the same time, the scope and scale of such differences is amplified by aspects that are present in print. Let us consider these now.

We can start with space. Print itself exists in finite space, but, more important, it also exists in a fixed relationship with space around it. You cannot have print without its space around it, and that interrelationship leads to important influences on meaning.

Used consciously, print space can and does convey meaning of its own. The amount and the location of such space can be used to precondition a consumer of print in such a way as to attach flavors of mood and emphasis to the body type it accompanies. Formality can be fostered by arranging space with mathematic precision and rigorous balance—as in the case of a well-printed bible. Frivolity and irreverence gain from balloons of space shaped in informal patterns, as is frequently the case in successful comic books.

Our focus, our expectations, and our pace can all be directed by such space. An experienced Print-English practitioner can use space to support and amplify on his print meaning in manners quite different from the oral-aural systems but quite comparable so far as effect and impact are concerned. Any deliberately designed newspaper page, for example, includes the use of space to preselect consumer attention and response. With remarkable accuracy, the choice of where you look, what you read, even what you will remember can actually be arranged. So too with magazines and books, posters and pamphlets.

Size is a companion factor. Variations in the size of type and in the size of accompanying pages or other settings are obvious devices used to amplify on the vocabulary and meaning of print. Simple shading of emphasis is provided by simple largeness (PAY ATTENTION!) and simple smallness (You Can Ignore This!). More sophisticated shadings emerge from interrelationships (THIS is more important than this but **MUCH LESS IMPORTANT THAN THIS!**).

We get a somewhat negative confirmation of this when contemplating misuses of size in print. Advertising that misses its target, for example, often makes the mistake of assigning size emphasis to the wrong words or the wrong relationships so that the combined size-content message does not ring true. And, as people literate in Print-English, we interpret and immediately dismiss such an obvious grammatical error.

Design is another important ingredient in the vocabulary of print. Through perceptive design, values, associations, amplified meaning, description, and many of the vexing abstractions of intangibility can be attached to Print-English. The shape and form of print can be orchestrated so that most impressions we intend can be conveyed. Even when alphanumeric intelligibility is totally lacking—as with the straight random lettering of a book of typefaces—meaning can be conveyed through typefaces alone (see fig. 1). We can be persuaded to read rapidly or slowly, to expect sobriety or silliness, to sympathize or resent—almost anything in the human lexicon can be fostered.

The design aspect of print is particularly striking because of its relative newness. Anyone familiar with early Print-English can testify to the barrenness occasioned by the absence of serious design considerations (see fig. 2). It is only in the last fifty years that extensive efforts have been made to relate the shape and form of print to intended meaning.

Ironically, this "newness" is probably quite relative. In previous incarnations—with the Chinese and various groups on the Indian subcontinent around A.D. 500, for example—forms of print were refined to include design considerations of a high order. Indeed, it is probably true that design has had to be rediscovered several times during the evolution of print, in much the same way that successive generations now labor to rediscover basic social values in contemporary society.

And there are still jokers. One minor discord in the Canadian celebration of centennial year in 1967 emerged when a noted print house decided to commission the design of a new typeface to honor the occasion and contribute to new and higher levels of easy reading. To their

FIG. 1.—Reprinted from *The New Literacy*, by Donald Gordon, by permission of University of Toronto Press. © University of Toronto Press, 1971.

DIAMONDS AND PEARLS.

DENIS JACOB begs leave to inform the Public, he gives the full value in ready money for Diamonds and Pearls, at No. 57, Margaret-street, Cavendish-square.

N. B. A variety of Articles in Diamonds and Pearls to be disposed of, second-hand.

Those who have not lately visited the Royal Menagerie, at Exeter 'Change, can scarcely form an idea of the perfection, beauty, and number of rare Animals it contains. It is unquestionably the most extensive and best conducted collection of living Curiosities in Europe, and reflects the highest honour on the spirited Proprietor, who has at such a liberal expence brought into one view the principal wonders of animated nature.

On the 1st of July was published, at R. Ackermann's, 101, Strand, London, SIX of the most interesting VIEWS OF CHELTENHAM, in Colours; size $10\frac{1}{2}$ by $7\frac{1}{2}$ inches. Price One Guinea.—To be had, at Cheltenham, of Mrs. Jones, Mr. Fasana, and Mr. Salmoni; and also at the shops of the two latter at Bath; and of all the Book and Print-sellers in the United Kingdom.—Also just published, as above, RURAL SPORTS, a Poem, by William Somerville, Author of The Chase, to which this forms a Companion;— with fifteen beautiful Wood Engravings, designed by Thurston, and engraved by C. Nesbit. Price, on English paper, 1l. 1s. in extra boards, and 1l. 11s. 6d. on India paper.

Silks and Satins, Black and White Square Lace Veils, Silk Shawls and Scarfs, Muslins, Lace, Hosiery, together with all such articles as are kept by the most respectable Silk Mercers, Drapers, Hosiers, Lacemen, and Haberdashers, 20,000l. in value, having been purchased in large lots, but will be sold in small or large quantities for the convenience of the Public, is offered to the Nobility and Gentry, of the best quality, which comprises all the novelty of the Season, at prices from 20 to 50 per cent. under regular trading houses; and to account for their cheapness, the whole were purchased from the ready manufacturers, and paid for on delivery at THOMAS's, of Fleet-street, West Corner of Chancery-lane.—N. B. Ladies or Gentlemen having commissions, will find this a very convenient resource. This Advertisement, to command immediate insertion, must be limited, therefore a detail of prices cannot be given.—No abatement will be made from a regular marked price, whether application be made by the connoisseur or the ignoramus.

SILK STOCKINGS

Are selling uncommonly cheap and good, at COOKE's Manufactory and Nottingham Warehouse, No. 434, Strand, near Old Round-court. The largest and most elegant assortment in the kingdom of all kinds of Hosiery, from the lowest to the very best that can possibly be made; Full Dress Silk Hose superior to any shop in London, and for evenness of quality not equalled; also a large quantity of Men's elastic Drawers and Under-Waistcoats; likewise Ladies Drawers, Under-Waistcoats, Petticoats, and Under-Dresses, all in one, both in Angola, Spanish Wool, and in Cotton. Drawers with feet; a great choice of Gloves of every sort, which are now selling on terms much more advantageous to the public than ever before offered, full 20 per Cent. cheaper than at any other house, wholesale, retail, and for exportation.—Goods made to any pattern.—N. B. An elegant assortment of black silk stockings of the first quality.

FIG. 2.—Reprinted from *Bell's Weekly Messenger*, July 18, 1813, p. 232

dismay, they found that readers gained their ease primarily from familiarity rather than design. So long as the typeface was known, the print form gained in legibility—all the strokes of master design could not facilitate legibility for a new typeface.

Further shadings of mood and meaning are to be found in the vehicle that carries English-Print messages. Be it paper or some alternative, the texture and color of the print vehicle can have a considerable influence. The effects are primarily those of mood—credibility, acceptability, and degree of seriousness, in particular. We are encouraged to trust, perhaps even worship, banker's parchment, to assign merit to scholar's onionskin, to assume the up-to-the-minute exhilaration of newsprint. Each time we bid to devise a Print-English expression, awareness of the vehicle must be included.

At this point, then, a Print-English language—vocabulary plus meaning attached to it—starts to become apparent and defensible as a concept. Any word or letter or number or other manifestation in the Print-English language comes to have meaning as itself plus space, size, design, and its vehicle (see fig. 3). Such meaning will be a specific and particular Print-English meaning different from other languages—including English or other solitary forms *and* including English-Film, English-Radio, or other compound media forms.

Furthermore, the English-Print language is also possessed of certain advantages of synthesis that should be taken into account. Not only is there a vocabulary of individual Print-English manifestations, there is also a vocabulary of combinations. Meanings that are both larger and often separate from individual meaning can be crafted from composites. Clumps of specific print can be sculpted in aggregates in concert with space, size, design, and available vehicles to convey overriding meaning—adding affirmation, raising questions, introducing denials, or whatever.

A page can have a meaning quite separate from its constituent words and other images. Aggregates of pages can have different meanings again. Aggregates of volumes can introduce even further combinations. Flat, basically two-dimensional Print-English can be synthesized into its own composite of expressions right to the very edge of three-dimensionality, perhaps even to the point of modified linearity.

As with any language, of course, the key to all this lies with the intent and competence of Print-English users. Provided we conceive of three-dimensionality and modified linearity and school ourselves to literacy in its composite expressions, the desired results can be achieved.

Consider advertising as an illustration. Much of the stretching and innovation (as well as the devaluation and dilution) of Print-English is to be found in contemporary advertising. And in advertising we find repeated instances of creative synthesis.

Individual words are shaped, sized, spaced, and placed astride special vehicles. They are combined in page patterns carrying overtones of

We used to be in a world of

UNITS

such as houses.

Increasingly, we are tumbling into a world of

aggregates

such as regional planning areas.

When it all works, we gain – as with streams, ponds, rivers, and lakes linked and laced into watersheds to provide an orchestration of pure, reliable, and joyous resources.

When something doesn't work, we lose – as when northeastern North America was plunged into darkness and hysteria for 18 hours in 1965 – the result of one fault in one power station that overloaded all the power networks in a regional grid.

Furthermore, some of the aggregates we live with come close to being ultimate. The consequences of the misuse of nuclear aggregates, for example, can be catastrophic. Our familiar Freudian friend, the automobile, may be purring and clanking a total transition to '1984.' Even the sensibly popular copulative aggregate needs to be eyed cautiously as a harbinger of constantly increasing population leading to global starvation.

Choice has become a premium fact in life.

→ Choice in terms of what to pay attention to.
→ Choice in terms of what to ignore.

Fig. 3.—Reprinted from *The New Literacy*, by Donald Gordon, by permission of University of Toronto Press. ©University of Toronto Press, 1971.

energy, sexuality, beauty, or even truth. They are linked to successive page patterns that start introducing flip-page reinforcement with the flavors of three-dimensionality and modified linearity. They are spaced over successive issues such as to challenge the strictures of time and fixed tempo.

Advertising's favorite concept—Sex—becomes "SEXY YOU NOW!" on a sensually active surface emphasized by suggestive colors, shapes, and spaces, designed in evocative forms, coded in thought-provoking sizes, reinforced by successive depths of pagination each with its differing perspectives, progressively loosening the jackets of order and logic, and pounding home with bludgeons of day-after-day, week-after-week, month-after-month amplifications.

Print-English, in sum, becomes quite a language!

Much of this, however, exists only as potential for Print-English in actual practice. The majority of print offerings make very, very little use of the opportunities available in the Print-English language. Ignorance, the chains of habit, and timidity combine to limit conscious formulations and experimentations and to blunt the thrust of accidental breakthroughs.

With most books, we wade through gray seas of type, routinely frustrated by the discord between form and content. The art and creativity implicit in a living language are seldom given the scope they need. The constrictions of largely mechanistic preoccupations squeeze, even obliterate the links of meaning that might enhance the total effect of a Print-English combination. It is rare indeed to find the full mutual reinforcement offered by the marriage of words with their setting.

The situation is somewhat better in other Print-English forms. Some magazines—*New York, Nova,* and *Realités,* for instance—demonstrate promising awareness of the powerful language they are working with. Some newspapers have begun to show signs of life too. And in the mountains of Print-English ephemera there are nuggets of literacy to be found.

But a lot remains to be done. Our relatively dim awareness, so recently gained, simply has to be improved upon.

And this brings us to our third step: formulation of guidelines for evaluation of print.

There are, of course, the conventional guidelines of literacy and excellence. Transferred from English to Print-English, such guidelines can be very helpful indeed, so long as they are not made absolute. Appropriate grammar, appropriate style, and appropriate syntax drawn from English usually serve to foster clarity and consistency of meaning in Print-English.

But some cautions and additions are also necessary.

First, we need to remember intent—both of the author and of the receiver. Unless evaluation takes intent into consideration, it runs the risk of being consumed by form at the expense of substance. As a gracefully retired Lady of Ill-Repute used to remind me, "Well, dearie, sometimes people do fuck," and any cosmetics applied in the cause of style or taste or the like cannot help but distort such intended meaning.

Second, we must constantly remind ourselves of the incompleteness of conventional guidelines. Print-English is a language on its own, possessed of pluses and minuses, as noted. Evaluation in terms of words, sentences, and paragraphs cannot cover the whole language of Print-English. And its focus on some portions may apply at the expense of the other parts and of the language as a whole.

And this, in turn, suggests the additions that we need.

We need to acknowledge and apply the guidelines of literacy and excellence to Print-English's other terms: literacy and excellence in the use of space, of size, of type design, of vehicles, and of combinations of all of these.

Then we approach mastery of the true grammar, style, and syntax of the Print-English language. We can enlarge our word, sentence, and paragraph conditioning to include consideration of appearance, setting, texture, and even color. We can consider total meaning.

This prospect cannot help but be exciting. It offers opportunities to facilitate the crucial business of human communication in a kind of language that persists in being the most pervasive in our world. It hints at exchanges enriched by quite remarkable improvements in mutual understanding. And it allows us, for a while at least, the luxury of making rules as well as memorizing them.

Try it.

THE TRANSFER FROM ONE MEDIUM TO ANOTHER: *THE MALTESE FALCON* FROM FICTION TO FILM

Virginia Wright Wexman

There is a well-known anecdote about the scripting of the 1941 film version of Dashiell Hammett's archetypal hard-boiled detective novel. John Huston, then a scriptwriter at Warner Brothers, convinced studio head Jack Warner to allow him to direct a third film version of *The Maltese Falcon*. Warner gave his consent with the stipulation that Huston work up an acceptable script for the project before he gave his final approval. The aspiring young director was to work with veteran writer Allen Rivkin on the scenario. The two scriptwriters decided that the most logical first step in the process of turning Hammett's novel into cinematic form would be to have their secretary type up the dialogue from the book, dividing it into scenes as it seemed appropriate.

The secretary followed her instructions faithfully. However, upon completing the manuscript, she sent it not to Huston and Rivkin but, by accident, to Warner himself. Warner, ironically enough, was delighted with this "adaptation." He called Huston into his office and insisted that the film be put into production at the earliest possible moment. Huston was astonished but hardly inclined to protest. So the unfortunate Allen Rivkin lost out on a potentially interesting writing assignment and John Huston prepared to direct a script which was undoubtedly among the most faithful adaptations of a fictional work in the history of cinema.

Though Huston subsequently made a few minor adjustments in his screenplay, the dialogue and action of the finished film are taken almost entirely from Hammett's novel. In part, this fidelity was possible because of the character of the original material. *The Maltese Falcon* lends itself wonderfully to the demands of film. It contains a great deal of action set in various locations around the city. With its detached, third-person point of view, it does not raise the awkward cinematic problem of portraying the thoughts of any of its characters: most of the action is narrated through crisp, witty dialogue. Moreover, Hammett's laconic style means that the atmosphere of the novel is not dependent on a rich verbal texture that might be difficult, if not impossible, to duplicate on the screen. The dialogue itself, though highly stylized, works well aurally as well as visually. Unlike the novels of authors such as Fitzgerald or Faulkner, *The Maltese Falcon* does not contain speeches which look beautiful on the printed page but which sound forced and stilted when read aloud. All of these qualities made Hammett's book an ideal choice for adaptation to the cinema.

In spite of the eminent filmability of Hammett's novel and the ease with which the initial screenplay was produced, *The Maltese Falcon,* like any other work of fiction, presented problems and challenges to its cinematic translators. To appreciate the qualities which contributed to the achievement of Huston's 1941 film, it is illuminating to examine the two earlier film versions, made in 1931 and 1936. Both of these adaptations suffered from an inhospitable social climate, undeveloped techniques and conventions within the film medium, and a lack of creativity on the part of the actors, directors, screenwriters, and others involved in the productions. As a result of these problems, both of these early versions fail in terms of what Erwin Panovsky calls "the principle of co-expressibility": the need for films to make their audio and visual components work together [1, p. 21]. Because film is a mixed medium, combining pictorial, dramatic, and musical elements in a mélange of sight and sound, each of its composite parts must be selected and shaped with an eye to how it can work with the others to produce a harmonious and unified overall effect. Hammett's novel, as we have seen, provided an excellent beginning point for this process. But it was up to the filmmakers to complement the dialogue and action they took from the book with an appropriate visual and aural style.

The 1931 *Maltese Falcon* (also called *Dangerous Female*) was directed by Roy Del Ruth. Like the later Huston version, the screenplay stays close to Hammett's original novel. But the dialogue that works so well in the book is not enough to ensure a successful film without support. In this first version of the *Falcon,* such support was too often uninspired.

A major problem of the Del Ruth adaptation was related to technical setbacks in the film medium occasioned by the advent of sound. In the early thirties, obsessed with the notion of the new talking pictures, Hollywood tended to devalue the importance of visual expression. Filmmaking ideas at that time often centered on getting hold of a script with striking, fast-paced dialogue which could be photographed in a simple, passive way. For many of the movie formulas of the thirties, such as the screwball comedy, this technique worked well. But the hard-boiled thriller required more visual atmosphere to create a mood of mystery and suspense. The pedestrian, thirties-style photography and even lighting setups used by Del Ruth on the 1931 *Maltese Falcon,* though well executed, cast Hammett's dialogue incongruously into the form of an urbane comedy rather than a tense melodrama.[1]

The sets and costumes used in Del Ruth's adaptation created further conflicts with the tone of the original literary material. Since thirties

---

1. This judgment of the 1931 version is not universally shared. John Baxter, in his book *Hollywood in the Thirties* [2], argues that the Del Ruth version is superior to the later Huston one because of its "polish" and its greater fidelity to Hammett's novel. It is difficult to understand the evidence on which the latter part of this judgment is based, and I would argue that the polished quality is at odds with the tough, thriller elements of the book. For Baxter's entire argument, see [2, pp. 200–202].

audiences went to films to escape the Depression-induced poverty of their real lives, Hollywood gratified their desires with luxuriously decorated sets and elaborate costuming. So Del Ruth's Sam Spade is the possessor of a paneled office and stylishly cut suits. Hammett's hero, by contrast, is a slightly down-at-the-heels marginal professional, a man whose life-style suggests that he is disdainful of the things money can buy. In rejecting the financial temptations offered him in the course of the story to "lay off the case," he proves that his personal integrity means more to him than material wealth. In Del Ruth's film, however, the attempts to bribe Spade lose their force, since he already appears to be a rich man. Hammett's portrait of a private eye whose personal style reveals him to be scornful of money and its benefits is completely buried in this interpretation.

The tone of sophisticated comedy which pervades Del Ruth's version of Hammett's book is further reinforced by the director's choice of actors. Ricardo Cortez, who plays Sam Spade, has a suave, Continental manner, and Bebe Daniels, as the "dangerous female," appears wholesome and relaxed too much of the time. Neither projects the nervous tension of Humphrey Bogart and Mary Astor in the Huston adaptation, a shortcoming aggravated by Del Ruth's predilection for shooting his stars in close-up. Again, Hammett's mood of ominousness and suspense is dissipated by a failure to make all the elements of the film work together according to Panovsky's principle of coexpressibility.

If the 1931 version of the *Falcon* watered down the impact of Hammett's original story with its pedestrian and urbane approach, the 1936 adaptation, directed by William Dieterle and entitled *Satan Met a Lady*, went to the opposite extreme, substituting an excessively bizarre and madcap style for the earlier bland treatment. This method proved even less successful than Del Ruth's had been. Here Hammett's dialogue and narrative logic are lost in an attempt to spice up the action and make it more visually exciting.

Brown Holmes, who worked on the screenplay for this version as well as Del Ruth's, evidently tried to vary the plot line and characterizations as much as possible so that the film would not seem simply a reworking of the 1931 *Falcon*. To this end, he changed the villainous fat man (played by Sydney Greenstreet in the Huston film) into a fat woman who was a notorious archcriminal. He also dropped the motif of the falcon completely in favor of a mystery involving a legendary horn filled with jewels. Such alterations destroyed the carefully controlled narrative of Hammett's original book without imposing any consistent point of view to replace it.

The violations of Hammett's intentions begun by Holmes were compounded by the directorial style of William Dieterle. Dierterle tried to give his film atmosphere by locating much of the action in outdoor settings, such as a foggy graveyard and a stormy waterfront at night. Such backdrops result in a loss of the claustrophobic intensity generated by Hammett's narrative, in which almost all of the action takes place indoors.

The casting and characterizations in *Satan Met a Lady* also reflect the filmmakers' determination to avoid the blandness of Del Ruth's earlier effort. Where Del Ruth's Sam Spade had been a prosperous, rather conventional businessman, Dieterle's version of the character, as interpreted by actor Warren William, made him out to be a flamboyant, irresponsible vagabond. William's Spade wore capes and wide-brimmed hats. He remained blithely unperturbed by the fact that he was continually being shunted from one town to another by irate citizens' groups. The sense of personal dignity exuded by Hammett's hero and the active pride he takes in his nonconformist values are completely missing in William's casual, devil-may-care portrayal.

Some of the other characterizations were equally miscalculated, especially the casting of Bette Davis as Spade's duplicitous woman client. Davis projects an image that is too strong and in control of things at all times for her to be convincing as the seemingly helpless and confused lady in distress. Dieterle's attempt to add an air of sprightly comedy to his film by casting affable Arthur Treacher and scatterbrained Marie Wilson in supporting roles had similarly unsatisfying results. One feels the tone of the movie as a whole continually wavering between that of a playful parody and a gothic thriller.

Though *Satan Met a Lady* substituted an excessively flamboyant style for the overly toned-down approach of the 1931 *Falcon*, neither film was able to adapt its cinematic techniques to the spirit of Hammett's story. One shortcoming common to both was a tendency to play up the hero's romantic entanglements. Such an emphasis was part of the comic feeling each film aimed for in its own way, but it detracted considerably from the audience's interest in the mystery of the falcon. Besides giving inordinate attention to the protagonist's romantic involvement with his enticing female client, both films soften the story's ending, in which Spade delivers her over to the police after confronting her with the fact that she has murdered his partner. The 1931 *Falcon* includes an epilogue in which Spade visits the disheartened villainess in prison and arranges to have the matron give her special attention and any amenities she might want. In the 1936 version, the concluding scene has Bette Davis calling gaily after Warren William, "The next woman you meet may be a little smarter than me: she'll marry you," as she is carried away by the police. Meanwhile, William saunters nonchalantly off in the opposite direction arm in arm with his secretary.

This alteration in Spade's character from a tough detective who solves crimes to a soft-hearted ladies' man is probably due for the most part to the temper of the times in which these two early versions of *The Maltese Falcon* were made. As a commercially oriented mass-entertainment industry, Hollywood has always been highly sensitive to the preferences of its public. There is a strongly misogynistic flavor to most hard-boiled stories that did not sit well with thirties audiences, whose taste ran to romance and happy endings in which the hero and heroine finally work out their differences. Sam Spade, as Hammett envisioned him in 1929, is a man who has an instinctive—and well-justified—suspicion of attractive women. In the thirties, however, when there was a deeply felt need for families to work together for better times, cinematic portrayals of women as untrustworthy villainesses were rare. In the prosperous forties, when independent women began to move into responsible male jobs as men went off to war, a vogue emerged for "femme fatales" in the movies: women whose sexual charms masked vicious and destructive designs. Mary Astor's Brigid O'Shaughnessy was perhaps the first of this cycle.

By 1941, then, the social climate was sympathetic to Hammett's story, with its emphasis on cynicism, nonconformity, hostility toward women, and contempt for materialistic standards. This sympathy, coupled with developments in film conventions and the fortuitous coming together of many creative talents, made possible *The Maltese Falcon* that most of us know today.

John Huston has said of his approach to adaptation, "I try to penetrate first to the basic idea of the book or the play, and then work with those ideas in cinematic terms."[2] In *The Maltese Falcon* he saw this basic idea as the mystery of the fabulous statuette of the falcon. Accordingly, he superimposed the titles of the film over the silhouette of the bird and added a brief written prologue describing its history before the action proper begins. He also added a line at the very end of the film in which his hero, in answer to a question about what the small black figure is, replies, "The stuff that dreams are made of."

Huston reinforced the mystery and suspense centering on the quest for the falcon by innovative lighting, sets, photography, sound, and editing. Unlike Del Ruth and Dieterle, who favored the even lighting techniques which were popular in the thirties, Huston lit his scences with harsh, uneven illumination creating bold, sharp contrasts between dark and light tones. The dark shadows add to the audience's sense of mystery, while the harsh black and white juxtapositions help to support the tough, uncompromising mood that was so much a part of Hammett's story.

The tough spirit of Hammett's book is reflected in the sets of the film as well. Spade's office and apartment are conspicuously shabby, befitting a man of proletarian background whose values do not include luxurious accoutrements. We can readily believe that the Sam Spade who occupies

---

2. Quoted in an interview with Huston by Gideon Bachmann first published in 1965 [3] and reprinted in 1967 [4, p. 257]. Pauline Kael makes an interesting argument against the view that Huston faithfully reproduced Hammett's intentions, since she sees a certain amount of irony toward Spade in the book which is not in the film. There is, in fact, some difference in the two artists in this area, but it is not one which is apparent to most people who see the film. (See [5, pp. 380–82] for an explication of this point of view.)

such an environment could have the strength of character not to lose his head in the scramble for the precious statuette as the other, wealth-addicted characters do.

If the search for the falcon tempts Spade to greed, it also threatens him with danger. We feel this danger throughout the action, in part because of the director's shooting style. Since Huston wants us to sympathize with his hero's nervous, volatile reaction to the threatening milieu around him, Spade is present in every one of the scenes, and each sequence is shot in a subjective way to suggest the emotional effect the action is having on him. Most of the shots in the film are taken from a slightly low angle from which the actors and sets appear to weigh down upon us. The overall mood is claustrophobic, though the precise effect of such shots is different in each scene. The villain Casper Gutman seen from a low angle, for instance, seems more formidably immense than he actually is. On the other hand, the first view of Brigid O'Shaughnessy as she timidly advances into Spade's office makes her appear on the verge of falling over because of the up-tilted angle from which we see her. Huston's photography thus immediately suggests her dangerous instability to us.

In the final scenes of the film especially, another aspect of Huston's shooting style adds noticeably to the feeling of danger generated by the action. With all the main characters assembled in Spade's apartment to await the delivery of the falcon, we see the action primarily in closely composed three-shots.[3] This method of shooting the group keeps us aware of the ever-increasing tensions and hostilities among its various members and the abrasive, potentially explosive effect this final coming together entails. Huston's method here is a vast improvement over that used by Del Ruth and Dieterle. Where Del Ruth's taste for close-ups of single actors breaks up the feeling of a group at war with one another, Dieterle's two-shots[4] disperse the conflict into various scattered squabbles. Only in Huston's film does the hostility generated in the group as a whole rise to a crescendo during the climactic final sequence in Spade's apartment.

Our sense of climactic finality in this last scene is further built up by Huston's ingenious use of editing and sound. The tedium and frustration of bargaining and waiting for the falcon is expressed in long takes.[5] When the statuette arrives, however, the pace changes abruptly, and the excitement connected with the unwrapping of the bird is suggested by a number of very brief takes in which various views of the action are intercut[6] in rapid succession. We see the falcon itself as it is clutched by the greedy hands of Gutman, Brigid, and Cairo. We are also given glimpses of the three adventurers leaning over the table from the per-

3. A three-shot is a view of three actors within a single frame.
4. A two-shot consists of two actors within a single frame.
5. A long take is an extended view of the action shot from a single camera position.
6. Intercutting is the process by which various views of an action or actions are edited together to achieve a kaleidoscopic effect.

spective of the package. Finally, Huston intersperses close-ups of Spade's face, alert and intensely curious in the background.

Roy Del Ruth's portrayal of the corresponding action in his own adaptation of the *Falcon* lacks the pace and power of the Huston scene, though it is made up of similar shots.[7] There is not so much cutting in the earlier version, for one thing, and the focus on the falcon is broken for a moment as Del Ruth pauses to show Wilmer, the gunman, taking advantage of his friends' preoccupation to make his escape through the window.

Huston controls the pace and tone of his film through sound as well as sight by a judicious use of background music, an element conspicuously absent from the earlier adaptations of Hammett's book. As the falcon stands unveiled, for instance, Adolph Deutsch's melodramatic theme rises in the background, adding to the impact of the moment aurally as well as visually. Throughout the film, Huston combines music on the sound track with careful editing to give his film rhythm and mood. Background music is such a crucial component of mystery-suspense movies that it is not surprising to find that few, if any, memorable films of this kind were produced during the thirties, since at that time the industry had not yet exploited the capacity of background music to coexpress the material presented visually and through dialogue.

Since Huston saw Hammett's story as a mystery-thriller, he played down the love story between Spade and Brigid O'Shaughnessy by means of clever camera work. Even the romantic scenes between the two are photographed so that they appear to us as part of the struggle to gain the falcon. When Spade first kisses his attractive client following his attempts to discover what sort of unpleasantness she is mixed up in, Huston shoots the incident from a low angle behind the hero's back. With his hands around Brigid's neck, Spade seems from this perspective almost as though he is physically bearing down on her in a effort to push out the desired information.

The second time the couple embrace, Huston follows Spade with a tracking shot[8] as he leans over Brigid's chair to kiss her. The camera then continues its track without pausing, past the two and over to the window behind them, where we see the figure of Wilmer waiting in the street below. Again, our attention is kept focused on the danger and intrigue surrounding the hero rather than on the pleasures associated with his love affair.

During the couple's final scene together, Brigid pleads with Sam to let her go free in spite of the fact that she has murdered his partner. As she kisses him for the last time, the camera views the action from a vantage

---

7. William K. Everson's excellent discussion of the three film versions of the *Falcon* points out that Huston must have screened the Del Ruth version at least once, since so many of his shots (including the one showing grasping hands) are quite similar [6].
8. A tracking shot is one in which the camera moves to follow the action instead of remaining in a fixed position.

point behind her and below eye level. The supplication implicit in this final gesture is thus emphasized as we see her body straining upward and directly away from the foreground of the frame. It is worth noting that this shot is a perfect complement to the earlier one of Spade kissing her for the first time, a shot taken from a similar vantage point behind him. The information he has been seeking from her has at last come out, and now, the camera tells us, she is in his power.

The way Huston handles the love relationship between Spade and Brigid, then, always emphasizes its connection with the mystery Spade is trying to solve, in contrast to the distracting treatments of this aspect of the story by Del Ruth and Dieterle. In this area, as in others, Huston was able to use the resources of film to express the melodramatic mystery story he saw in Hammett's work.

Probably the single most celebrated aspect of the 1941 *Maltese Falcon* is its casting: Sydney Greenstreet as Casper Gutman, the fat man; Elisha Cook, Jr., as his bodyguard, Wilmer; Peter Lorre as the childish, effeminate Joel Cairo; Mary Astor as Brigid O'Shaughnessy, the seemingly helpless female who is revealed as a murderess; and, of course, as Sam Spade, Humphrey Bogart, the man Howard Hawks has called "the most insolent presence on the American screen."[9] Huston's casting is so uncannily effective that some critics, such as Andrew Sarris, have attributed the success of the film entirely to the director's skill in this area alone [7, p. 156]. The characterizations become even more impressive when one realizes that it was in this film that Lorre, Greenstreet, Cook, and Bogart first established the movie personas they have been known by ever since. In the case of Bogart, the role marked his emergence as the major Hollywood personality of the forties. In the words of French film historian Georges Sadoul, "Humphrey Bogart was well known as an actor at the time, but this film was really the first to introduce the famous 'Bogie' characteristics that made him a star" [8, p. 206].

It is worth noting that Bogart was physically very unlike the character originally projected by Hammett. The Sam Spade of the novel is tall and fair-haired. In a film, though, the hero Hammett describes would not have worked effectively with the fast-talking and arrogant figure the dialogue and action suggest. Bogart's height was ideal for the role of the hard-boiled detective. He was not as tall as western heroes like John Wayne and Gary Cooper, who convey a certain moral superiority merely by virtue of their towering stature. But he was not as short as gangster heroes like James Cagney and Edward G. Robinson, who appear visually at a disadvantage with everyone else and whose contentious temperaments invariably set them at odds with the world around them. Bogart was of average height: short enough to share some of the gangster's pugnaciousness but tall enough to partake in some of the western hero's

---

9. Spoken on the PBS-TV production of "The Men Who Made the Movies" (section on Howard Hawks) produced by Richard Schickel.

dignity. In addition, his wiry build gave him the fast-moving agility we associate with urban film heroes. He was not classically handsome in a conformist, matinee-idol way, and his dark coloring and heavy features gave a suggestion of ethnicity to his appearance. These characteristics reinforced Spade's image as a tough, independent proletarian. Finally, the dissipated look of Bogart's face gave his hard-boiled detective the air of a man who had experienced life in some of its more unsavory aspects.

Bogart's qualifications for the role of Sam Spade extended beyond the physical attributes he brought to the part. His acting style and manner also contributed to the success of his characterization. His diction was well suited to the tough-guy image, combining lower-class intonation with a lisping, nasal edge that bespoke a disillusionment with what the world had to offer. Bogart customarily delivered his lines with a good deal of nervous energy, but there was always a humorous, mocking air about him that made him appear above the vicissitudes which enmeshed the other characters. Then, too, he employed a variety of visual mannerisms that suggested an intelligent man struggling with a difficult problem: stroking his jaw, pulling on his ear, hitching up his trousers, raising the sides of his upper lip, lighting a cigarette. Such gestures repeatedly draw our attention to Bogart's mental efforts to solve the mystery of the falcon. With remarkable economy, they continually remind us that Spade is a thoughtful man, intent on unraveling the threads of the plot for us.

Though Bogart received his initial training as an actor on the stage, his style was better suited to the cinema, where close-ups could capture his subtle use of gesture and expression. More importantly, Bogart's style was eminently cinematic in that he exploited and coexpressed the physical qualities of voice and appearance he brought to the screen with his acting methods. In many ways the role of Sam Spade represented an ideal coming together of actor and character. Tough, cynical, independent, volatile, wryly humorous, and at last alone with his own integrity, the character of Sam Spade merged irrevocably with the star persona of Bogart in Huston's film.

Bogart's phenomenal success in the role of Sam Spade emphasizes the different means which sometimes must be used in film to achieve an emotional effect on the audience similar to that evoked by the original fictional source material. Where Hammett's Spade works well in the novel as a tall, fair-haired man, it is doubtful that such a figure on the screen could have projected the tough, proletarian image audiences saw in Bogart, an image that is necessary for an adequate cinematic realization of Hammett's intention. In this, as in other elements of Huston's production, the problem was to recreate the feeling generated by the book in terms of the various elements of film: camera work, lighting, editing, sound, acting, set decoration, and costuming. As is clear from the failure of Roy Del Ruth's adaptation, mechanical fidelity to the action and dialogue is not sufficient in itself; the filmmaker must be prepared to think in terms of realizing the spirit of the original work in cinematic terms, changing details when it seems desirable. From this perspective, Huston's revisualization of Hammett's hero, which preserves the unity and force of the novel, is clearly a change of a different order from the many arbitrary and frivolous alterations made in the 1936 Dieterle adaptation of *The Maltese Falcon*.

In each of the three film versions of Hammett's book, it is clear that considerations relating to audience prejudices and the particular individuals involved in the productions had a considerable influence on the form the material finally took. The problem was not only one of transposing the story to the film medium; it was also one of finding the right people to do it and of producing it at a time when public tastes would not conflict with the values Hammett envisioned. The success of the 1941 *Maltese Falcon* is due to the confluence of first-rate screen material, hospitable social conditions, technical advances within the medium itself, and creative genius. The last of these factors is represented most notably by Huston and Bogart, one interpreting the action of Hammett's novel and the other his protagonist.

The process of creation is, at bottom, a similar one in all forms of artistic endeavor. The goal is to create a lively and unified work. In a book it is necessary to match—or coexpress—the action with appropriate language, style, rhetoric, and the like, to achieve this goal. In film, the question of coexpressibility involves the manipulation of other elements besides verbal ones, but the final product must be judged on its own merits using the same kinds of aesthetic standards as would be used for literature. A great film, like a great novel, is the product of a sophisticated artistic sensibility. Such a sensibility is best described and evaluated by responsible and informed critics thoroughly trained in the elements of the particular art form they are analyzing. All communication media which have an aesthetic dimension demand special talents and skills of both creative artists and critics. A respect for these special talents and skills is our best guarantee of quality in any of the media.

REFERENCES

1. Panovsky, Erwin. "Style and Medium in the Motion Pictures." Reprinted in *Film: An Anthology*. Edited by Daniel Talbot. Berkeley and Los Angeles: University of California Press, 1966.
2. Baxter, John. *Hollywood in the Thirties*. New York: Paperback Library, 1970.
3. *Film Quarterly* 19, no. 1 (Fall 1965): 3–13.
4. Sarris, Andrew. *Interviews with Film Directors*. New York: Avon Books, 1967.
5. Kael, Pauline. *Kiss Kiss Bang Bang*. New York: Bantam Books, 1969.
6. Everson, William K. *The Detective in Film*. Secaucus, N.J.: Citadel Press, 1972.
7. Sarris, Andrew. *The American Cinema*. New York: E. P. Dutton & Co., 1968.
8. Sadoul, Georges. *Dictionary of Films*. Translated by Peter Morris. Berkeley and Los Angeles: University of California Press, 1965.

ADMINISTRATIVE PROBLEMS AND THEIR SOLUTIONS

Wesley Doak

I would like to begin by telling you a little about the objective of this paper and the objective of my work as a library consultant for the California State Library. They are, in fact, exactly the same. I like to think of all forms of public administration, including library administration, as being vehicles for answering human needs. We spend a lot of time analyzing the methodology, and, of course, this must be so. As I talk with librarians about the manner in which they can best achieve the administration of a wide range of library resources, I try to keep in mind that the objective is simply giving our users the information they need in the form they can most readily use and retain for their personal satisfaction. It is very easy for all of us under the pressures of lack of space, lack of money, and lack of adequate personnel to begin thinking of solutions to these separate problems rather than aggressively putting together a package that will think of the user first.

As this paper progresses I plan to cite a few examples of how we as library professionals have managed some of the other recent developments in the library world, then move on to an analysis of how we have thus far been managing media, and finally to make some constructive suggestions for ways to improve on where we are now.

Looking at the broad perspective of recent library advances, one might conclude that there are two major changes going on presently that are rapidly changing the face of libraries. One is the subject at hand —the influx of nontraditional library resources. The other is automation with its electronic data processing, computers, on-line terminals, data files, and sundry printouts. The fact is that both of these relatively quiet revolutions are part of libraries' efforts to become more fiscally and socially responsible. While automation is not today's subject, it does have some relevance to the concerns of the conference. I think a quick look at that aspect of the current library scene can show us some of our weaknesses as a profession as well as some of our strengths.

I would like you to think for a moment of any libraries you know which are using some form of automated procedures. Can you think of many, or, for that matter, can you think of any, that are using such technology to do anything other than to automate existing manual processes? My work probably takes me to more libraries in a month than most of you get to visit in a year, but I would imagine that your conclusions would be the same as mine. It is almost sad to be taken on a visit by a proud librarian who informs me that his library can check out books, clear the record upon their return, take reserves, send overdue notices, and order materials through his new system. My first reaction to that, although usually unspoken, is: You could do all that before you automated, probably cheaper, and maybe faster. Some libraries and library systems *have* used the fantastic facilities in the computer age to bring on-line bibliographic searches to their users, to create entirely new data files, and otherwise to expand library resources rather than simply redoing the old. However, creating new uses of computer technology is not today's subject either. Creative management of media is. The sole reason I mentioned automation is to bring home a point that is equally true in the field of the media as it is in automation. Most recent research in media administration is undertaken to see how we can improve existing patterns of audiovisual services. Taking my cue from the Fenwick and Asheim writings about this conference, I would like today to look at the characteristics of current media administration and then evaluate how they contribute to, or obstruct, if that be the case, better total service for libraries.

In summing up what I have said thus far, I would like to think I have made clear my own first rule, if you will, of administering media in libraries. That is: completely rethink your whole philosophy of multimedia service. Do not assume that improving the existing plan of service is the only answer. One cannot assume that improving what one has will be any solution at all.

After all, what is "audiovisual"? Administratively some have played a variation on the old game of "animal, vegetable, or mineral." Their modern version is something like "subject, service, or program." I would like to begin by pointing out some ways that library administrators have thought of audiovisual materials. One of the ways was to have "audiovisual" as a subject department. You have seen libraries like that —with a History Department, a Science and Technology Department, a Religion and Philosophy Department, etc., and along with these, a department entitled Audiovisual. Actually, audiovisual materials belong in all those subject departments, do they not?

A second popular way of organizing "audiovisual" into the library administrative pattern is to call it a type of service. You have Children's Services, Young-Adult Services, Adult Services, Out-Reach Services, and on and on they go; and one of those is Audiovisual Services. But, audiovisual materials and services should be part of every one of those types of services, should they not?

The latest insult was perpetrated by a so-called consultant firm that thinks "audiovisual" is a type of program. They list acquisitions, cataloging and classification, interlibrary loan, reference, etc., and one program is audiovisual. Obviously audiovisual materials fit into, or require, all those types of library programs, too. A major change in the philosophy of administering new media is needed. Audiovisual materials are a type of resource, not a subject, not a type of service, and not a type of program!

My second rule for good media administration is one that Dr. Asheim alluded to in his introductory essay, and that is to expect the very same quality of service in audiovisual or newer media as you would of the best service in traditional media. In a moment I will be more specific, but by this last statement I simply mean that there is no excuse for lower standards for audiovisual services and resources than one sets for "book" services and resources.

Modern management practices and principles give us many formulas and even more catchy phrases to explain the processes whereby goods, services, information, and other outputs of government can be analyzed. It has been around for awhile now, but management by objectives is still a growing practice. The scientific or "one best way" method is certainly not dead, as I will demonstrate, and there are a growing number of individuals who ascribe to the "if it feels good, do it" principle, attempting to throw out every rule that slows down progress toward whatever it is they feel is important in public service. My contention is that, while there is no one best way to administer or manage book *and* nonbook, audiovisual, or instructional media in every instance, we have tried a number of methods at length that are not working, and we would be wise to discard those in many circumstances.

George Odiorne, a former Peter Drucker pupil and now a popular speaker on management by objectives, states that "tasks go from being an idea to an element in a job description to a specialty, to a profession, and finally, to a religion" (to use his description loosely). This sad story is in fact what has happened to the concept or idea of using the most useful information resources wherever they are most appropriate; to the now too-regimented, almost religious devotion to audiovisual communication. It is not a religion, it is not a secret power that one possesses, it is not a gift one is given or not given. To my way of thinking, having a completely separate audiovisual department in one's library or school is no different than having a separate one for paperbacks, or oversized books, or books with large type. Some people think that is a bit harsh, but I think not. This parallel does point out, however, that we do need to think about such resources, plan for them, budget for them, possibly buy special shelving and other equipment for them, and certainly promote their use to the proper group. You will find that I do consider audiovisual materials unique, special, and, most of all, essential to the operation of any information-gathering and disseminating agency, whether it is called a library, media center, or a community information center. I just find that when they are treated with too much reverence, given special people to run their activities, separate catalogs, etc., we collectively lose our ability to serve the people who need that special information most.

Let us take a few minutes to look at a list of common library activities. In each case we will then explore the reputation, deserved or undeserved, of audiovisual media. Activity number 1 is budgeting and acceptance. Can it be said that in most libraries audiovisual materials get their just share? Can it be said that library resources reflect the needs of the user community? Are audiovisual materials considered basic library resources or are they considered a unique resource? Are they considered audiovisual aids or something else?

The second activity I would like to take a quick look at is acquisitions. Are all library resources a part of the main acquisition system? If so, have they been incorporated into the normal procedures or do they require a long list of special rules?

Cataloging and classification is the third library activity I would like to examine briefly. Are users of nonprint media second-class citizens when they walk up to a card catalog or when they open a book catalog? Are we anywhere near the day when an information seeker can look up a subject or an author/performer entry and expect to find all the library's holdings conveniently displayed for his selection?

How about technical and mechanical processing? A library would not think of not putting a shiny new cover on books, reinforcing spines, or pocketing maps and other extra materials that are enclosed with the traditional media. How often, though, have we seen records simply dumped in a bin and looking so motley that they would not intrigue anyone but the most die-hard and needy of audio users?

The fifth item on the list would be storage and retrieval. Again, as we look at the present tradition of administering a multimedia library we must ask ourselves, are the storage and retrieval methods for audiovisual materials as efficient as they are for traditional materials? Have libraries planned for, appropriated, and budgeted proper shelving, proper booking systems, on-line search capabilities?

The sixth is repair and maintenance. How often do we find film collections with banged-up cans and scratched and sprocketed footage because of poor technical and mechanical processing of these valuable resources?

Next we need to look at staffing patterns. How many times have you observed that the newest staff member in a public library as an example, gets "stuck" with the job of the audiovisual section? How many school librarians are forced to become the media-center director when they already are the librarian? Worse yet, how many school libraries are staffed by teachers on the bottom of the totem pole, so to speak, rather than having a properly trained librarian on duty at all times?

The eighth item concerns itself with the use and programming of audiovisual materials. As I talk to school and college leaders I find that, more and more, the average classroom teacher or professor is not asking for the use of the production facilities. The responsibility for production is going to a person who has as his or her sole responsibility the production of instructional materials. In public libraries it is common to find that only the audiovisual librarian or department is programming for nonprint media. There are exceptions of course, and to a great extent we might say that the exceptions are growing rapidly. But, even in what I am calling exceptions, they tend to be in the areas of children's and young-adult services. It is still a certain exception to the rule when, in a public library, a department head for business and industry, or a department head for science and technology, or a general reference staff will use any nonprint media as program elements.

The ninth activity would be community or user public relations. It is fashionable to include the words "film" or "records" in public relations releases for libraries. I am glad to see this growing trend even though in some cases there is not much of that kind of material available when the user shows up to take advantage of what has been offered. However, we do not need to look very far—only to the recent National Library Week and its slogan, "Be all you can be, read"—to learn that in the public relations area we still have not told people that the medium *they* use most (when they are not in the library) is in fact available if they should care to come to their school or public library.

There are a great many other categories we could go through like this, including allocation of space and an item I mentioned briefly before —the use of nonprint media and on-line services—such as OCLC, Library of Congress MARC, or ballots[1] types of program. But I think we have established that in most fundamental activities of libraries audiovisual materials are not an integral part of the scene. In other words we have not expected or attained the same level of service for nonbook materials as we have for the traditional media.

Of course the above list is not necessarily in order of importance, nor do I mean to imply that they are all always separate functions. But I do think we can isolate them enough to evaluate each in the light of current media administration. It seems to me from this quick analysis that if budgeting, acceptance, acquisition, and the other things I mentioned all lack the true incorporation of nonprint media as smoothly running elements of their activities, we can hardly assume that we are providing the full range of media to our users. In a moment I am going to attempt to show why this has happened. If we can isolate a cause and suggest a cure, we will have begun to solve the problem of media administration.

As you know, schools for quite some time have planned an organized way to deliver various combinations of their resources to students in an attempt either to teach students or let them teach themselves. This rather precise, although not altogether agreed-upon science, is called instructional technology. I would like to suggest that the methodology used by instructors could be used by librarians in planning and then rating their own ability to administer audiovisual materials in libraries. There is one major difference in the plan that must be brought up once again. Instructors in a school situation do the deciding on what is to be taught; the math teacher upon arriving in the classroom does not expect

---

1. A library system for computer-based data processing developed at Stanford University.

to find the students awaiting a lesson in football pass patterns. However, a reference librarian or library administrator upon greeting a library user gets no such advantage, and, in fact, does have to wait for the other party to announce the topic for investigation. In this sense, we cannot program specific titles ahead of time. However, most other aspects of the comparison do have considerable validity. We as librarians can look at the same four areas of administration that the instructional technologist uses to devise a good program: (1) what goals are to be accomplished? (2) how and under what circumstances will users (in their case usually students) seek to accomplish goals? (3) what resources will be needed to organize library materials to aid users in reaching these goals? and (4)—one that we all slack on quite a bit—how well were the goals accomplished? Now that sounds simple enough, but there are seven steps required to accomplish answers to these four questions: (1) devise or accept objectives, (2) list activities that will accomplish them, (3) determine which media will be necessary to carry on those activities, (4) plan physical facilities that are necessary, (5) appropriate suitable staff to man the facilities, (6) obtain the materials and equipment, and (7) evaluate the program against the objectives listed in item 1.

Let us go over that list of library activities I mentioned earlier and ask ourselves whether or not we have achieved equal or at least commensurate status with traditional media. Budgeting? Acquisitions? Cataloging? Classification? Technical Processing? Storage? Retrieval? Repair? Maintenance? Staffing? Programming? Space? Public Relations? We could go on. I think it is fair to say that few of you hearing this talk this morning (or reading the paper) would be able to say that audiovisual media get their just share. The facts are that in most cases every category I listed exposes the second-class citizenship among media of the so-called nonprint formats.

I would also imagine that there are some of you in the audience today and among the readership of the papers presented at this conference who would say it took me a long time to point out something that most of us who are interested in true multimedia librarianship have already known. That is the fact that in most cases the nonprint media have a second-class status, whether in school, higher education, public, special, or other library scenes. And if we want to correct the situation—if we want to see libraries of all kinds collecting resources and using them efficiently—if we want, even more important than either of those two things, to have *users* in various communities that we serve able to come to a library and go away satisfied because we have really given them what they needed in a format they can understand and use, we have to know not just that there is a problem, but why.

So far I have tried to show some reasons why we are in this particular state. I think that we can clearly lay the blame for high costs and the second-class citizenship of some of the newer media specifically on the traditional means of administering them. Some media fanatics would see the problem as the responsibility of library administrators and of school administrators. Their contention is that the administrators do not understand the new media and do not care about them. I reject this as being blatantly false in most cases. I do know that there are some people who are unfamiliar with audiovisual materials and resources, but I have rarely found a person who did not want to know more about them even when he felt he had no expertise in these matters.

There is another school of thought that says that it is the public that really does not want the newer media, and I think that this is blatantly false, too. One needs only to look at circulation figures in any library, large or small, since the advent of audio recordings and motion-picture film in readily usable format, or to look at audience participation in film programs, to see that users in schools and public libraries do want a full range of media. I would expect that all of you already agree with that too. Again, who is the culprit? I know my answer will sound ironic to some, but I think that by and large the major cause of poor audiovisual service is simply separate audiovisual or instructional technology departments.

Here briefly are some rules that I strongly urge you to consider if you want to improve the media administration in your school or public library. (1) If you do not have a separate audiovisual or instructional resources department in your institution, do not start one. (2) If you do have such a department now, get rid of it as soon as possible. (3) Make everyone in your organization—and I do mean everyone—equally responsible for all information resources. (I might add here that I see nothing wrong with having a coordinator who would aid in developing this responsibility or in budget preparation, especially in the early days of the new service. However, one such position even in the largest of libraries would be sufficient to improve audiovisual service enormously. This position should not be a permanent one and, I would hope, not employed on the local level. Once there is a department, the rest of the staff often put their own responsibilities in total media matters out of their minds. And, as someone mentioned yesterday over lunch, the specialist gets more and more specialized and pretty soon will not touch anything if it is not 16mm, or if it is not audio, etc. I am not trying to make fun of all media specialists, but what I have described is, unfortunately, part of the true picture of media specialists at their worst.) (4) Make familiarity with the newer media and skill in their use part of the rating and reviewing system for personal advancement. And, (5) incorporate all library resources into one centralized access vehicle that could be a book catalog, card catalog, data terminal, or any other process that gets total library resources to the user without the traditional resource-hunt routine. I have no objection to separate catalogs if they are an addition to a complete one; in fact, I would encourage that.

If an objective of full library service is to try in every case to provide resources in their best medium, the library cannot afford to have an audiovisual department, at least not in the traditional sense. No one librarian or department can choose the appropriate media for all subject areas and all age levels and all types of services. The Children's Department, for example, must select its own resources including books, magazines, motion pictures, toys, games, filmstrips, models, audiovisual recordings, and—if they are available—wacky-packs. The department head knows best what is needed. Maybe the greatest loss in the separate-system approach is the fact that when staff are not involved in selection, they almost invariably remain among the nonusers of audiovisual media. That same principle applies to every department in the library that buys library material. If the branch librarian, the department head, the outreach coordinator, the individual teachers, do not actually participate in the selection and acquisition of the newer media, these media will not be used to their full potential. I firmly believe that anyone who is constantly looking at school and public libraries and rating them would tell you that this is a rule almost without exception.

The problem with the "separate but equal" audiovisual department is that its clientele often sees these materials as merely an arts-and-crafts alternative to the commercial cinema, a way to avoid making a speech or devising a creative program, or a method for keeping a schoolroom quiet on Friday afternoons. A realistic and honest view of many audiovisual programs, when they are separate that is, would indicate that their services are not even remotely tied to the libraries' overall plan of service. Their collections do not remotely indicate the ethnic, religious, social, and educational needs of their communities. What keeps them funded and going in most cases? Basically, the old measuring stick of circulation figures. Many administrators can only show a circulation increase by incorporating audiovisual materials into the total library statistics. Films, recordings, videotapes, and the like are very popular. A library administrator looking for some underpinning in these times of shrinking funding sources is not likely to tamper with this most popular circulation-building activity. But, he or she should!

So much for identifying problem areas. A few words about possible solutions. Let us just take one more look at that list of library activities, now in the light of the five rules for good administration of total library resources that I mentioned earlier. Let us ask ourselves if it is reasonable to assume that giant strides could not be taken toward user satisfaction, lower costs, and higher staff involvement if we could get rid of the concept that the audiovisual services are in the same category as services to special users, identified by age levels or some other distinguishing characteristic requiring separate treatment.

First, budgeting and acceptability. I have already seen this concept in action many times; when every department head, every age-level service coordinator, every teacher, and every librarian is responsible for developing a true multimedia program rather than relying on some person down on the first floor, or up on the eighth floor, or over in another building, their selection improves, and their budget for audiovisual materials doubles or triples almost immediately. Of course, this also means a really invigorated image of the library for the student in the school library or for the public library user.

Second, if the acquisition department had the responsibility for ordering all library resources, it would not be long until those processes were ironed out. When the film librarian insists on doing his or her own ordering (I do not mean selection) and the record librarian insists on doing his or her own ordering, we simply multiply our costs and delay the day when acquisition of all resources is a smoothly running and normal procedure for everyone concerned.

The third area was classification and cataloging. The advent of library cooperatives, library networks and systems, and computerized data bases for the exchange of information has rapidly pulled this particular aspect of audiovisual materials into the mainstream. However, again, laying the blame at the feet of the "audiovisual as a segregated function" addicts, I must say that had they not insisted on their own cataloging and classification schemes (with an occasional valid exception such as Bro-Darts ANSCR),[2] had they not insisted on their own separate catalogs and similar procedures, etc., cataloging departments in libraries would long ago have been putting all the library resources into the best form for their users. Technical and mechanical processing suffers from the same problem. The facts are that once those departments accept the burden of processing recordings, films, filmstrips, video, and all the other audio and visual media, it will work smoothly there too.

When every department is liable for the storage and retrieval of total resources, there is an immediate and profound change in the attitude about where certain materials can be housed. Repair and maintenance have just as interesting a pattern when all library staff members become involved. Books and audiovisual materials are seen in a new light. All over the country there are film libraries, for example, which sorely need electronic inspection and cleaning units to keep their collections in top shape. The fact is that as a rule only one or two of the staff members ever have to face the patron who could not get the film to project, or a record to play, or a cassette to turn; therefore, it is hard to get an item like a cleaning unit or film-inspection unit through the normal budgetary processes. The simple fact is that when most of the staff are isolated from this kind of need, they have no way of putting it into perspective in terms of the library's budgetary priorities.

The same thing is true in space and staffing. Once everyone in the organization is equally responsible for all information resources, it is no longer a matter of a media freak trying to take valuable space from books, or, conversely, having a film collection moved time and time

---

2. A cataloging, classifying, and/or processing service for audiorecordings developed by the Bro-Dart Foundation and available through the Bro-Dart library supply firm.

again because of the need for more stack areas. Maybe best of all is the fact that once everyone is involved in the processes of selection, programming, and utilization of audiovisual materials, our users gain as much as, and probably more than, we do.

I mentioned earlier that there are at least seven steps required to accomplish really first-rate administration of total library resources. I would like to go over at least some of them again in view of the hard-line approach in the current scene to separate administration for some media to see whether, in applying those seven steps, we can come up with the same answer we did when we simply looked at general library activities and asked ourselves whether or not we were happy with our findings.

You will recall that the first step was to devise or accept objectives. We might translate this into how audiovisual materials fit into what have traditionally been called book-selection policies. Frequently the library's objectives are clearly written. At least, the book-selection policy is written, and sometimes a plan of service has also been put into written form. But I find that many times only "the names have been changed to protect the innocent." Dr. Henne in her paper mentioned that in library-school classes, book-selection techniques are retitled materials-selection techniques with little change in actual content. I am afraid the same thing happens in libraries and schools when it comes to "materials"-selection policies, yet often all that is needed is a section stating the relevance of certain media to content.

The second step was to list the activities that would accomplish the objectives of the library. Of course that pertains primarily to what I mentioned before in the plan of service. Again the important element is to recognize that all media have their places, and that we cannot have a library that is limited to audiovisual materials only, any more than we can have a full library service that is limited only to books.

Third was to determine which media would be necessary to carry on those activities. Obviously every library does not need every form of audiovisual resource.

The fourth item was to plan physical facilities that are necessary; the fifth was to obtain appropriate staff to look after the resources and the facilities and program. And the final two elements in the seven steps to accomplish good library administration were to acquire the materials and related equipment and to evaluate the program as a whole against the objectives that were laid out in the selection policy and the plan of service.

Can anyone honestly say that a single individual, however talented, however dedicated, however motivated to providing audiovisual service, can actually accomplish these seven steps on a library-wide basis? That is why I state that a library with a separate audiovisual department can never provide first-class library service. This is not to say, however, that they were never needed, and this is an important point to me, for in fact some of the really outstanding people who have managed such departments have made monumental contributions to the growth of libraries as true multimedia agencies. My contention is simply that the need for that kind of separated administration is by and large already past. The longer we cling to that style of managing different media, the longer it will be before we really have first-rate service for all of our users.

Libraries of all sorts have the same natural enemies that all public administration units face. One is the straight competition for tax dollars. The school library may be competing with the athletic department for money, and regularly does; the public library may be competing with the police department, etc. The second form of competition is in the realm of similar services. As an example, we often find that school and public libraries are competing with each other as to who is giving students the major part of the service they need. But we also find that the corner paperback bookstore, the television screen, the daily newspaper, the radio, the special library, are actively competing with us and with each other in the fight for survival. There have been so many surveys of how people find help or get information, how they spend their money and their leisure time, how they rate their civic services, that no further justification seems necessary for libraries developing programs which will make them become more popular, if we intend to survive as free-to-the-public, yet tax-supported, institutions.

In summation, I would just like to say that if you want to improve your administrative ability for all media you must keep two general principles in mind. The first is, as I stated before, rethink your whole philosophy of multimedia service. Do not assume that improving your existing plan of service is the only answer. Second, expect the very same quality of service, audiovisual or newer media, as you would of the best of service in the traditional media. If you conscientiously apply these two concepts to your library, I think you will come up with the same conclusions that more and more libraries and librarians around the world are coming to, and these are, as I stated before, (1) if you do not have an audiovisual or separate instructional resources department, do not start one; (2) if you have such a department now, get rid of it as soon as possible; (3) make everyone in your organization equally responsible for all information resources; (4) make familiarity and utilization of skill with media part of the rating and reviewing system for personal advancement; and (5) incorporate all library resources into one access vehicle.

The results will be higher budgets for resources, lower administrative costs, higher staff involvement, and best of all, vastly improved service for library users!

SUMMARY

Sara I. Fenwick

From time to time in the history of these annual conferences it has seemed useful to use a summary at the close, especially where, as in this one, a variety of aspects of a subject, cutting across several professional interests, have been presented by experts in fields that in some cases are only tangentially related to the day-to-day activities of librarians. Every member of this audience is the center of a variety of activities concerned with media which generate special and individual needs, and no single topic can be all things to all people. Because of this diversity of approach it seemed that it might be useful, on this occasion, to pull together some of the threads from the papers which have been presented during the past two days.

It was our hope at the outset to offer participants—while listening to speakers who have thought seriously about some of the facets of the messages of certain media and how those messages are recorded, transmitted, and received—an opportunity to arrive at some of the principles that differentiate the characteristics and potential ability of each medium to respond to various needs of the several publics the participants serve.

The papers were planned to examine a few representative samples of a quite extensive group of packages of man's recorded knowledge, no one of which, in itself, is peculiar to a library, but the aggregate of which forms the physical resources of a library. And our particular approach to these packages was prompted by a concern, not for their shape or wrappings or delivery, but for their content and the standards by which we can judge the significance and worth of each to men's needs for knowledge, inspiration, and understanding.

We recognized from the beginning that there would be many in this audience who would have overwhelmingly important needs for guidance in how to acquire, organize, administer, and utilize the mass of media with which a librarian is faced, and to whom this concentration of program time on the characteristics that determine the effectiveness of a few of the media would seem impractical and irrelevant. Therefore, it seemed useful to identify some of the generalizations by which we have tried to differentiate a few of the media, in the hope that this process will be useful in dealing with other media we have not recognized within the scope of this Conference.

It is unlikely that the ideas that one person has listened to and pondered with greatest interest will necessarily be those of first importance to each one in the audience, but it is hoped that these generalizations will suggest some useful and continuing confrontations with communications needs of your own.

In his introduction Lester Asheim identified the focus of the Conference as the identification of characteristics—technological, aesthetic, social, and psychological—that determine the effectiveness of each medium for different kinds of users and purposes. He spurred our motivation to recognize the factors involved in evaluation by emphasizing that a film, book, recording, or other medium accomplished the creator's purpose only to the degree that the potential of the medium was realized effectively.

Our several speakers have given us some guidance in recognizing the characteristics that determine effectiveness. As we have considered these factors, those who are librarians have been particularly conscious that they are doing so in relationship to their responsibility to act as mediators for the communication needs of the library's various publics. Let me recall some of the comments and discussion addressed to the general problem of evaluation.

Repeated several times in various ways was the basic principle that the medium tends to impose its own nature on the content. Virginia Wexman testified to this as she documented the processes of change with techniques of illuminating, obscuring, emphasizing, that are inevitable in translating content from one medium to another.

Ron Powers juxtaposed three media with similar content but each with a different effect upon the receiver. While the personal subjective approach was noted as a significant factor, there was, nevertheless, recognized by the receiver and by this audience, a quite different experience in the three encounters with the same content. It was obvious that the quality of each experience was affected by the nature of the medium.

Donald Gordon discussed the principle in terms of print—alerting us to the constraints imposed by its linearity, but also to the new dimensions that modify this inherent characteristic of print.

A term that was used by more than one of the speakers, and one that we are becoming accustomed to using in a very broad sense today, is *language,* used to describe the ways—not necessarily verbal—by which the several creative contributors to a production present the content. We continue to recognize as language the vocabulary that is employed, the way in which the vocabulary is used, and the meaning it carries, but today's broader usage no longer limits vocabulary to vocables. It is a sobering thought to consider the number of languages in which all who deal with communications media need to develop a proficiency today.

Donald Gordon's dramatic differentiation of the language of print, as opposed to the oral-aural language, established for us that print has a language with elements that interpret and go beyond the letter symbols. Space, size, pace, and design in the use of print are some of the elements in this language.

That film could be called multilingual seems to be inferred from Virginia Wexman's demonstration that the camera, in every medium in which it is the instrument, speaks in a language richly its own, but also that the music, the set decoration, the cutting, the costuming are elements in film language that give meaning to the content.

We can continue to use these two media, print and film, not as opposite ends of the spectrum of communication media, but as forms removed some distance from each other, in order to abstract some guidelines for evaluation that identify the elements to look for in developing a functional literacy. As we consider the medium of print, we add to our traditional evaluation of the quality of the author's use of words to record his content—syntax, grammar, and style—a sensitivity to, and an appreciation of, the language of Print-English. The understanding of this language comes from the perception of elements of space, type size and design, page design, paper characteristics, or other receiving vehicles which aid in arriving at the whole meaning of what the print says about the content. (As an aside, it occurred to me that it is possible to recognize that Print-English has had a considerable impact on the television medium as one watches "Sesame Street" or "The Electric Company," and one can wonder whether children today are being conditioned to a more sensitive response to the language of print.)

For the evaluation of film we need to develop a literacy that sees and responds critically to the language of camera angles, lighting, music, appropriateness of setting, of costuming, of social milieu, and the effect of all these elements on character interpretation as it is orchestrated by the pace and rhythm of the editorial cutting. All of these language elements should add up to Panovsky's *coexpressibility* as interpreted by Mrs. Wexman.

In the medium of film, because we are dealing so frequently with translations from another medium, it is necessary to seek particularly what Mrs. Wexman referred to as the basic theme or spirit of the original production. This principle does not translate as suggesting that mere faithfulness in replicating every aspect of the original work is necessarily the mark of a good film translation of a work of fiction, but rather that the consistency and unity, as well as the essential idea of the original work should, be evident.

There are many questions to be posed regarding translations. Mrs. Wexman emphasized the importance of the effect that the differing social climates had upon the three translations of *The Maltese Falcon*. How does the filmmaker assess the role and response of the receiver of the translated communication? Should adaptations to conform to a social or national mood inevitably be made, and accepted by critics, as being more relevant to the audience? And if the role of the audience is a murky one, what of the creator-author-playwright-artist? Would he have said the same things in another time or setting? What would his own creative language be in another medium? It can be granted that in the case of a piece of fiction—if it has a well-motivated plot, strong characterizations, and a theme of significance—those elements can be translated into any medium and carry some insurance of providing a good production in the standards of the second medium, but the treatment of the content in a different language may convey a significantly different meaning.

Perhaps some light is thrown upon these questions in an account of the translation of a picture book into an animated film by the artist himself. This was an experience of the illustrator Blair Lent [1]. He discovered one principle very early in his work when it became apparent to him that he could not simply repeat the book's illustrations even in animation on the film because of the viewer's need to be able to look at faces and details closely. With the book, the reader could shift his own position and set his own pace—page by page; for the film the camera had to share in the selection and emphasis and pace. As the creation of the film progressed, new characters—creatures in a procession—appeared, and the illustrator tells us that the movement of the figures actually suggested new plot directions. New scenes were created, and new facets of characters' personalities seemed to develop. But in the editing the creator was again concerned that he not depart too far from the simplicity of the original picture book.

In an indirect way all participants in this Conference recognized that the languages in which we communicate professionally are recognized as problems of education for librarianship. Frances Henne reminded us in various contexts of the accelerating need for the preparation of both media specialists and media generalists. Few library educators and administrators would argue that our rate of progress is anything other than "glacial," as Miss Henne termed it. Our past response, little changed in practice in the present, has been to compensate for our lack of language facility in the full range of media by turning to the specialist—first of all to the specialist in technology, and less frequently to the findings of research in psychology, linguistics, education, and aesthetics. In the larger libraries of all types, a considerable advance has been made with current patterns of differentiated staffing that have brought to the aid of the media generalist the skills of the television specialist, the photographer, the graphic arts specialist. But we have been reminded by Wesley Doak that there is a need for this relation to operate in both directions: the subject specialist, department head, teacher, and librarian should have a filtering, interpreting role to play in designing and facilitating the routes of access, the indexing, and the programming of the content.

Wesley Doak has interpreted our concern with differentiating the media in a fundamental way by alerting us to the all-to-common treatment of the audiovisual media as a separate administrative unit, a circumscribed body of skills and knowledge, and, therefore, a department or an assignment in the library organization. In library education this interpretation takes the form of a separate course in audiovisual materials in the library. To provide for the services of the media generalist, as defined by Frances Henne, it seems obvious that every librarian must be willing to accept the responsibility that such a role entails. To the extent that he can broaden his command of the languages of communication and his abilities to respond to a variety of media, he should be able to perform his role as a filter for the whole range of communications. This does not mean he must perform as a creator or a specialist in all the technology of all media, but rather as a reference librarian, a children's librarian, a cataloger, a systems librarian, a school librarian, a department head, a supervisor or coordinator, to be able to set objectives for the accessibility and utilization of all media and to interpret them in terms of users' needs.

As a footnote to Mr. Doak's paper, there is a development in the planning of collections in school media centers that is apparent in the frequently gradual transformation of book-centered libraries, particularly in schools and in education departments of academic libraries, into media centers. From a study of exemplary and typical secondary school media centers by Mary V. Gaver of Rutgers University in 1969 [2], it was found that a majority of the media center directors agreed that to inaugurate the expansion of a book-centered library into a media center, it was preferable to begin with one new medium at a time, planning for growth by adding other media gradually. This principle of collection development was retested in 1974 by Gaver with a sample of secondary school media directors in the United States and Canada, and revisions in the principle were made to the effect that it is preferable to begin with a few specific curriculum subject areas and with teachers' aid select a variety of media to support instruction in these areas.

In all the Conference discussion periods there seemed to be a productive concentration on the content of the media as opposed to the container. It is reasonable to conclude that the section of Frances Henne's comprehensive paper dealing with the subject of container orientation identified the current status and shape of the future to the extent that participants could put aside habitual visual and operational preoccupation with containers.

Another aspect of the discussions was related to the multilingual world we live in. As professionals, we spend a great deal of time in meetings and conferences on the top of a Tower of Babel of our own creating. It seems worth remarking upon that participants could talk and listen together with so little semantic difficulty—at least manifest semantic difficulty—obstructing our pursuit of ideas. We all know that in our several subprofessional alliances in the communications field we communicate in a variety of tongues, born of our collective efforts to differentiate—not the media, in most cases—but the professional responsibilities associated with the media. These languages serve useful purposes in helping the practitioner define and recognize the specific attributes of his task, but they are also stumbling blocks to communication with other professionals, and sometimes become the vehicle of frozen stereotypes in professional talking and writing. There was little evidence of this particular obstacle to communication in this Conference. Problems of understanding only made an appearance when the discussion was in the area of organization and administration of services.

In our summaries, we should not lose sight of the emphasis that was placed by Frances Henne and Ron Powers particularly, but by all of the speakers generally, on the need for more research, demonstration, and experimentation in the needs and responses of users of communication, in the optimum development of bibliographical access, and in the development of examination and reviewing apparatus.

Northrup Frye has used some wise words about language in writing in another context about the education of the imagination: "People who call themselves humanists, and include students of literature, have always been primarily people who studied other languages ... the humanists have always insisted that you don't learn to think wholly from language; you learn to think better from linguistic conflict, from bounding one language off another" [3, pp. 118–19]. Frye continues to speak of the constructive power of the mind in the imagination and the units it works with: "The units don't have to be words: they can be numbers or tones or colors or bricks or pieces of marble. It is hardly possible to understand what the imagination is doing with words without seeing how it operates with some of these other units" [3, pp. 119–20].

It was with some of these other units that the papers in this Conference were concerned, and they have indeed helped us to a better understanding of what the imagination does with words as well.

REFERENCES

1. Lent, Blair. "How the Sun and the Moon Got into a Film." *Horn Book Magazine* (December 1971), pp. 589–96.
2. Gaver, Mary Virginia. *Services of Secondary School Media Centers: Evaluation and Development.* Chicago: American Library Association, 1971.
3. Frye, Northrup. *The Educated Imagination.* Bloomington: Indiana University Press, 1964.

THE CONTRIBUTORS

LESTER ASHEIM: William Rand Kenan, Jr., Professor of Library Service, School of Library Science, University of North Carolina, Chapel Hill. Born Spokane, Washington, 1914. B.A., University of Washington, 1936; B.A.L.S., University of Washington, 1937; M.A., University of Washington, 1941; Ph.D., University of Chicago, 1949. Dean and associate professor, Graduate Library School, University of Chicago, 1952-61; director, International Relations Office, American Library Association, 1961-66; director, Office for Library Education, American Library Association, 1966-71; professor, Graduate Library School, University of Chicago, 1971-74. Publications include *A Forum on the Public Library Inquiry* (ed.) (New York: Columbia University Press, 1949); *The Core of Education for Librarianship* (Chicago: American Library Association, 1954); *The Future of the Book* (ed.) (Chicago: University of Chicago Press, 1955); *New Directions in Public Library Development* (ed.) (Chicago: University of Chicago Press, 1957); *The Humanities and the Library* (Chicago: American Library Association, 1957); *Persistent Issues in American Librarianship* (ed.) (Chicago: University of Chicago Press, 1960); *Librarianship in the Developing Countries* (Urbana: University of Illinois Press, 1966); and numerous articles in scholarly periodicals.

WESLEY A. DOAK: library consultant, California State Library, Sacramento. Born Oberlin, Ohio, 1939. B.A., Yankton College, 1962; M.L.S., University of Massachusetts, 1963; currently working on a master's degree in public administration at California State University, Sacramento. Fine arts and audiovisual librarian, Cary Memorial Library, Lexington, Massachusetts, 1960-63; librarian, Monterey Park Public Library, 1966-68; assistant director of audiovisual services, Los Angeles Public Library, 1968-73. Founder and coeditor of the *Film Review Index* and the *International Index to Multi-Media Information*.

SARA I. FENWICK: professor, Graduate Library School, University of Chicago. Born Lima, Ohio, 1908. B.A., Case Western Reserve University, 1931; M.A., University of Chicago, 1951. Assistant to children's librarian, young people's librarian, and head of work with children, Wilkes-Barre, Pennsylvania, Public Library, 1931-44; assistant to director of work with children, Enoch Pratt Free Library, Baltimore, 1944-46; head of work with children, Gary, Indiana, Public Library, 1946-49; elementary school librarian, Laboratory School, University of Chicago, 1949-56; since 1956 a member of the faculty of the Graduate Library School, University of Chicago. Publications include *New Definitions of School Library Service* (ed.) (Chicago: University of Chicago Press, 1960); *School and Children's Libraries in Australia* (Melbourne: F. W. Cheshire, 1966); *A Critical Approach to Children's Literature* (ed.) (Chicago: University of Chicago Press, 1966); and numerous articles in scholarly periodicals.

DONALD R. GORDON: associate professor, communications studies, University of Waterloo, Canada. Born Toronto, Canada, 1929. B.A., Queen's University, 1953; M.A., University of Toronto, 1955; attended London School of Economics, 1956-63. European correspondent, Canadian Broadcasting Corporation, 1957–63; assistant professor, department of political science, University of Calgary, 1963–65; associate professor, department of political science, University of Calgary, 1965–66; assistant professor, department of political science, University of Waterloo, 1966–67; associate professor, University of Waterloo, 1967–71. Publications include *Language, Logic and the Mass Media* (Toronto: Holt, Rinehart & Winston, 1966); *The New Literacy* (Toronto: University of Toronto Press, 1971); and articles in scholarly periodicals.

FRANCES HENNE: professor, School of Library Service, Columbia University. Born 1906. B.A., University of Illinois, 1929; M.A., University of Illinois, 1934; B.S. in library science, Columbia University, 1935. Member, New York Regents Advisory Council on Libraries, 1964–74; chairman, Joint Standards Committee of the American Association of School Librarians and the Department of Audiovisual Instruction of the National Education Association, 1969; vice-chairman, Executive Committee of the Educational Media Selection Centers Project, 1971–73. Publications include numerous articles on librarianship and education published in scholarly periodicals.

RON POWERS: television critic, Chicago *Sun-Times*.

VIRGINIA WRIGHT WEXMAN: coproducer, "Perspectives," Radio and Television Office, University of Chicago, and visiting lecturer, Department of English, University of Illinois, Chicago Circle campus. Born Winnipeg, Canada, 1941. B.A., University of Chicago, 1970; M.A., University of Chicago, 1971; Ph.D., University of Chicago, 1974. Lecturer in fine arts, University of Chicago Extension Division, 1972–74. Publications include "The Case for Pop Architecture," *Soundings* (Fall 1968); "The Role of Structure in *Tom Sawyer* and *Huckleberry Finn*," *American Literary Realism, 1870–1910* (Spring 1973); and "Character, Action and Style in Ingmar Bergman's *The Touch*," *Focus!* (Spring 1973).